PORTRAITS OF JEWS

ABRAHAM TOURO

GILBERT STUART

Owned by The Ehrich Galleries, New York

Portraits of Jews

BY GILBERT STUART AND OTHER EARLY AMERICAN ARTISTS

BY

HANNAH R. LONDON

WITH AN APPRECIATION BY
DR. A. S. W. ROSENBACH

AND AN INTRODUCTION BY
LAWRENCE PARK

CHARLES E. TUTTLE COMPANY: PUBLISHERS
RUTLAND, VERMONT

Representatives
Continental Europe: BOXERBOOKS, INC., *Zurich*
British Isles: PRENTICE-HALL INTERNATIONAL, INC., *London*
Australasia: PAUL FLESCH & CO., PTY. LTD., *Melbourne*
Canada: M. G. HURTIG LTD., *Edmonton*

Published by the Charles E. Tuttle Company, Inc.
of Rutland, Vermont & Tokyo, Japan
with editorial offices at Suido 1-chome, 2-6
Bunkyo-ku, Tokyo, Japan

Copyright in Japan, 1969 by Charles E. Tuttle Co., Inc.

Library of Congress Catalog Card No. 69-19613

Standard Book No. 8048 0459-1

First Tuttle edition published 1969

PRINTED IN JAPAN

TO MY PARENTS

CONTENTS

LIST OF PLATES

PUBLISHER'S FOREWORD

THERE are many reasons why this reprint of Hannah R. London's *Portraits of Jews by Gilbert Stuart and Other Early American Artists* is important, but the chief ones are that it depicts the not inconsiderable role these Jewish families played in the history and development of Colonial America, and it points up the great debt these artists owe to their Jewish patrons.

It is not illogical to conclude that through the early recognition of Gilbert Stuart's genius by these Jews, the artist received the early impetus that propelled him rapidly to fame and fortune. Thus it was with many other early American artists who received encouragement and inspiration from their Jewish patrons.

The author, Mrs. B. M. Siegel in private life, is justly called "the foremost living authority on American silhouettes," an art form she discusses in her book. Her work has won praise from Bernard Berenson, the foremost art critic of his day, who wrote of her book: "It is interesting, informing, and stimulating," and added that he was interested in the history of the infiltration of the Jewish element into American life.

Mrs. Siegel's book does indeed reveal indirectly the infiltration of the Jewish element into the mainstream of American life, and for this as well as other reasons her book is a very important contribution to Americana and the rich American heritage.

ERRATA

Page, 20

1778 has been given as the date for the death of Rabbi Karigal, but 1777 appears on the canvas of his portrait at upper right where the inscription should read:

"Rabbi Raphael Haijm Isaack Karigal;
  born at Hebron; educated there &
  in Jerusalem; died at Barbadoes
    AETAT.... MDCCLXXVII."

Page, 66   ADDENDA, under Jacob H. Lazarus
  Mrs. Mordecai M. Noah should read:

Mrs. Manuel Noah (Zipporah Phillips), 1764–1792. Mother of Major Mordecai M. Noah.

ADDITIONAL INFORMATION

Portraits of the Franks family are now thought to be by Gerardus Duyckinck I, 1695–1746.
See: "Mezzotint Prototypes of Colonial Portraiture: A Survey Based on the Research of Waldron Phoenix Belknap, Jr." by Charles Coleman Sellers. —*The Art Quarterly,* Vol. XX No. 4 Winter, 1957.

AN APPRECIATION

THE work of Mrs. Hannah London Siegel on the portraits of Jews in America from Colonial times is not only a most valuable contribution to the history of the Jews in the United States, but also supplies a considerable addition to our knowledge of early American artists. Mrs. Siegel is the first to treat this interesting subject in a comprehensive way. The fifty-eight illustrations which the author has supplied, after a laborious and thorough search, are invaluable. Mrs. Siegel has visited the descendants of Jewish Colonial families and what she has discovered is a veritable treasure trove. She has revealed to us for the first time portraits by eminent American artists which we did not know were in existence, and others of which we had record, and their early history, but did not know their present location. The reproductions form a veritable Jewish Colonial Gallery, and we can now behold the very lineaments of the early worthies who founded the first synagogues and charitable organizations; who fought in the early wars; who were active in the first explorations of the West; and who did so much in a patriotic sense for the country of their adoption.

The reproductions consist of some of the finest work of John Wollaston, Samuel King, Charles Willson Peale, Rembrandt Peale, William Henry Brown, Jeremiah Theus, Charles Peale Polk, Robert Feke, James Sharples, Benjamin Trott, Fevret de St. Mémin, and John Wesley Jarvis. There are no less than twelve portraits by Gilbert Stuart listed in the text, and twenty-six by Thomas Sully. The exquisite miniatures painted by Edward Greene Malbone are also mentioned, as well as silhouettes and drawings by other artists.

It is to be hoped that students will take advantage of this mine of new material so delightfully unearthed by Mrs. Siegel, and that collectors of Early American Portraits will be inspired to nobler efforts in the future; that a definitive work on the whole subject of our early Portraiture, like Lawrence Park's on Gilbert Stuart, will some day be given to the world.

A. S. W. ROSENBACH.

INTRODUCTORY NOTE

ALTHOUGH something had already been done in a fragmentary way to preserve a record of Colonial Jewish portraiture, the pages which follow are the first results of much deeper research in this field. They represent pioneer work of a peculiar interest, for in Colonial times the comparatively few Hebrew families along the coast were eminent in commerce and scholarship, men and women whose faces show great strength of character and often beauty of feature. They were, in fact, a picked racial group, usually, perhaps always, of the Spanish and Portuguese strains.

These people, as Mrs. Siegel has pointed out, encouraged artists by commissions, and to them Gilbert Stuart was indebted in his early Newport life, while in the career of Thomas Sully the Jewish group is a pronounced factor, including, as it does, the famous Gratz family of Philadelphia, by whom Stuart was also employed.

It will be a surprise to the uninformed reader to learn that these Jewish families, highly respected, wealthy, and patrons of art, were scattered throughout the seaports of the Atlantic coast, in Newport, New York, Norfolk, Savannah, Charleston, and New Orleans. This means that from Stuart in New England to Theus in South Carolina most of our artists of this period are represented. Copley forms a rather striking exception, which I can account for only from the fact that the Jewish element in Boston was a negligible one during Copley's active life.

Without the portraits here described our art would have been less vivid and picturesque, just as without these Jewish leaders American commerce and society would have been the poorer, while the history of Colonial and Early American art is much indebted to Mrs. Siegel for the results of her work.

LAWRENCE PARK

PREFACE

THE study of the portraits of the early American Jews suggested itself to me while assisting Mr. Frank W. Bayley in the arrangement of an exhibition of photographs from the portraits of Gilbert Stuart, at the Copley Gallery in Boston, in the spring of 1920. Here, among the hundreds of reproductions hanging on the walls, was a photograph of the portrait of Samuel Myers, the original of which is owned by a descendant, Mrs. John Hill Morgan, of Brooklyn. The writer, as a matter of curiosity, felt impelled to discover if there were other Jews who were patrons of art in the days preceding the Revolution and during the period of the early Republic.

As there is little published material relating to this subject, no pretence is made to having covered it comprehensively. In the main I have been dependent upon such fortuitous sources as notes in diaries, random passages in forgotten volumes, references from friend to friend, and correspondence in this country and abroad— London, particularly, where there are still illimitable sources for research. An account of these portraits was first presented in some papers which I read before the American Jewish Historical Society at Philadelphia, 1921, and in New York, 1922. The interest evoked at these meetings brought forth much additional information, which is embodied in the following pages.

In the preparation of this work I am thankful in no small degree for the help and encouragement of many friends; to Mr. Frank

W. Bayley, who gave generously of his time on the many occasions when I stepped into his gallery to chat over some new find; to Mr. John Hill Morgan, a busy attorney, but never too rushed to ride his special hobby on the field of early Americana; to the late Lawrence Park, with whom I had the privilege of exchanging information on the Stuart portraits of the Jews; to Mr. Samuel Oppenheim, a careful student of early American Jewish history, for his painstaking efforts with the proof, and for his valuable corrections and suggestions; to Mr. Lee M. Friedman, Mr. Charles K. Bolton, Dr. Cyrus Adler, Mr. Leon Huhner, and to Dr. A. S. W. Rosenbach, in whom there was ever a listening ear and a buoyant and unflagging interest. My thanks are especially due to my husband, Benjamin Mordecai Siegel, to my sister, Bessie London Pouzzner, and to her husband, the late Benjamin S. Pouzzner, for reading the manuscript, for their helpful suggestions, and for their constant encouragement which inspired the furtherance of this work. And lastly, I am immeasurably grateful to those who have given me biographical data and the permission to illustrate from their precious portraits.

Some of my articles on this subject, together with illustrations, have appeared in the following publications: *American Jewish Year Book*, volume 25, 1923–1924; *The Menorah Journal*, February, 1925; *Daughters of the American Revolution Magazine*, February, April and December, 1926.

CAMBRIDGE, June, 1926

I

SOME MISCELLANEOUS PORTRAITS

AMONG the earliest examples of portraiture in this country are those of a number of Jewish settlers who came here from Portugal, Holland, Germany and England in the decades preceding the Revolution. The fact that they have been unknown and withheld for so many years from general knowledge is not perhaps as strange as it might seem. For, in the first place, the little band of Newport Jews who came to America, like the Puritans, to escape persecution, and who found here a haven, carried with them an instinctive desire to shield their private lives from the public glare and calumny to which they had been so pitilessly exposed in their previous abodes. Relatively few in numbers, they became, as time went on and events hurried on one another with dramatic intensity, so completely identified with the life of their time that there did not seem to be a need of making separate note of their lives or portraits. As some of these families have died out, however, in the course of years, and as others have become disintegrated or lost sight of through intermarriage, it seemed a pity not to make permanent record, before it was too late, of these early Jews who from the beginning played a significant part in the history of this country, who by their patronage and innate love of beauty fostered the growth of American art and whose portraits are among the most treasured possessions of their Jewish and Christian descendants.

It is, moreover, only within the last generation that there has been a revival of early Americana sufficient to attract general attention. In this revival public interest has been quickened by the numerous exhibitions which have been held from time to time, including a wide range of artists, from Copley to Stuart, from Smibert to Sully. Many of the artists represented in this group painted the portraits of contemporary Jews. It is much to be lamented, however, that as yet I have not discovered a portrait of an American Jew by Copley. While in England in the spring of 1921, I happened on a portrait of Dr. Samuel de Falk, a Rabbi, which Copley painted on his return to England at the outbreak of the Revolution. If Copley found a patron in him, it is not unreasonable to infer that he may have painted portraits of other Jews living in England at that time, including those who returned to England with the not inconsiderable number of loyalists who left the colonies at the outbreak of the Revolution.

The collection of the Hon. N. Taylor Phillips, of New York, contains a number of the earliest examples of Jewish portraiture in this country, for the most part unattributed. One of these is the portrait of Jacob Franks, who was born in London in 1688. It is probable that he accompanied Moses Levy to New York about 1695. He later married Levy's daughter, Bilhah Abigail. Franks was a prominent merchant and became a freeman of the city of New York, August 21, 1711. His intellectual interests were not a few. He was a master of many languages, a fluent writer, and learned in the Jewish law. He had the degree of Rabbi of Divinity, and was known in the Congregation Shearith Israel by the title of Rabbi. Upon the erection of a new synagogue to take the place of the old frame building on Mill Street, the oldest place of Jewish worship in New York, he superintended all the details of the construction of the building and assisted in raising funds. He also gave generously to other denominations, and among these gifts was a contribution to build the steeple of Trinity Church, New York. At his death on January 16, 1769, the Pennsylvania *Gazette* of January 26, 1769, gave out the following notice:

Last Monday morning died at an advanced age, Mr. Jacob Franks, for many years an eminent merchant of this city. A gentleman of most amiable character; in his family a tender and kind master; as a merchant upright and punctual in all his dealings; as a citizen humane and benevolent, a friend to the poor of all denominations; affable and friendly in his behaviour to all. He is now gone to receive from the supreme God whom he adored his reward among the faithful. The memorial of the righteous is blessed. On Tuesday his remains were decently interred in the Jews' burying place, attended by a great number of friends.

Franks was buried in the cemetery of the Shearith Israel Congregation on New Bowery, New York.

His portrait is life-size and full length. Standing, he is turned three-quarters toward his right, with his face almost front. His right hand, palm upward, and with index finger well extended, rests on a pedestal, while his left hand rests upon a table draped in large folds of red and blue, which fall from the curtain in the left background. His ruddy complexion is offset by a powdered wig and a white neckcloth, folded over under the chin. His brown collarless coat has long sleeves and deep cuffs topped off with buttons. At his wrists appear the white muslin puffs of his undersleeves. In spite of its austerity, and its naïveté of treatment, the portrait has a dignity and calm characteristic of many of the attempts of early American painters.

Mr. Phillips owns a very charming portrait of Bilhah Abigail
Franks, the wife of Jacob Franks, and daughter of Moses Levy.
She is seated, turned slightly toward her left, in a life-size portrait
with her dark brown eyes facing front. She wears a gayly colored
blue dress with a voluminous skirt. Her bodice, cut low at the
neck, is held together at the breast and over the shoulders by or-
namental clasps, and reveals an underblouse of white silk with
elbow-length sleeves. Her right hand rests on her lap, and her left
elbow rests on a table, draped in red, with the hand hanging. The
face is soft and gracious. Her dark hair, brought tight behind the
ears, is parted in the middle, with a curl quaintly tossed over her
left shoulder. At the left of the canvas are clustering trees with
sky and clouds overhead.

Mrs. Franks worked zealously with her husband in behalf of
their communal and religious interests, and helped him to secure
funds for the erection of the synagogue by enlisting the services of
the ladies of the congregation. Under her direction every Jewess
in New York contributed; where money was not available, trinkets
and jewelry which could be converted were received. The synagogue was finally dedicated in 1730.

Mrs. Franks' devotion has not been forgotten. Her work is
recognized by a separate prayer, recited in her memory—now for
two hundred years—by the Shearith Israel Congregation, on the
anniversary of the consecration of the synagogue, on the Day of
Atonement, and on the anniversary of her death.

Their son and daughter, David and Phila Franks, are also represented in two sets of portraits painted when they were children.

In the painting which has been photographed, David is shown
standing full length, turned toward his right, and with his eyes

directed to the spectator. He wears a collarless blue broadcloth coat with wide cuffs and breeches, and a long full skirted waistcoat with small buttons. About his throat is a white neckcloth with a white muslin shirt ruffle. His right hand rests on his hip, while a bird, jaunty and defiant, perches on the index finger of his left hand. The pallor of his face is enhanced by the dark hair which falls easily about his head. His sister, Phila, sits beside him. Though only two years his junior, the artist indicates a greater disparity of age. She wears a little white dress, cut low at the neck, and with full elbow sleeves, over which a red scarf, probably a studio property, is carelessly thrown. Her legs are crossed and from under her dress slightly extends a little bare foot. Her rather cheery expression indicates her pleasure in being painted together with her older brother. The background is a neutral wall with an opening at the right showing the trunks of high trees, topped with foliage, and woods in the distance.

The other painting of David and Phila shows David standing with his right hand on his hip and wearing the same costume as above. Phila wears a red dress and holds a lamb in her lap while extending a rose to her brother.

There is another painting of Phila as a young lady in a life-size portrait, sitting, and turned slightly toward the right while facing front. A red scarf is thrown over the right shoulder of her blue dress, and held in place by her left arm, rests upon her lap. A loose-fitting bodice shows the soft ruffles of her chemisette at the neck and elbows. Piquant, yet demure, is Phila's appearance with her dark hair parted in the middle, and a curl quaintly tossed over each shoulder, and holding in the crook of her elbow a basket of flowers, lightly supported by her left hand. The landscape background is rather elaborate, showing large trees to the left and a low garden wall silhouetted against some clustering cedars.

David and Phila were constantly in the society of the well-known people of their day, and although their parents were devout Jews, they married outside of their faith.

Phila, born in 1722 in New York City, became the wife of Oliver De Lancey, who was born in New York in 1717. He was the eldest son of Stephen De Lancey and Ann Van Cortlandt. At the outbreak of the Revolution he adhered to the Crown, raised a corps of provincials called the De Lancey Battalions, and was appointed Brigadier-General. Their home, now known as a public house—Fraunces Tavern—still stands on Broad and Pearl Streets, New York City. Some notable events took place in that house. There the New York Chamber of Commerce was founded in 1768, and after the Revolution, it was the scene of General Washington's celebrated Farewell Address.

By the act of 1779, General De Lancey's property was confiscated, and his family journeyed to England, where they remained. General De Lancey died at Beverly, October 27, 1785, and was buried in the choir of the cathedral of that place. It is not known when Phila died, but it is believed that she survived him. Their children married very distinguished people in England, as we shall see in the following letter written to me by Mrs. Charles Rieman, of Baltimore, who is a direct descendant of Phila's aunt, Rachel Levy:

A daughter, Susan, of General and Mrs. De Lancey, married Lieutenant-General Sir William Draper, of the British Army. The second daughter, Charlotte, married Field Marshall Sir David Mendes, Commander-in-Chief of the British Army. The third daughter married Colonel John Harris Cruger. The eldest son was Stephen De Lancey. He was Lieutenant-Colonel of one of the three regiments known as the De Lancey Battalions, and after the Revolution was successively the Crown's Chief Justice of the Bahamas, and Royal Governor of Tabago. Stephen De Lancey had a most distinguished son, Sir William Howe De Lancey, K.C.B., the "Great Duke's" Quartermaster General at Waterloo, 1815. The second son of Phila and General De Lancey was Oliver, Jr., Lieutenant-General in the British Army and Member of Parliament in 1796. With him ended the male branch of the De Lancey family.

Among the descendants of the De Lancey family in England, some interesting portraits are doubtless to be found; perhaps another painting of Phila, and also portraits of Jewish friends she must have known in England, who, like herself, went back to the mother country because of the Revolution.

David Franks, Phila's brother, as I previously mentioned, was painted twice with his sister. He was born in 1720 and married Margaret Evans in 1743. David organized a military company in New York City about 1745. He later removed to Philadelphia, where he was one of the most prominent members of Philadelphia society. His home was the Logan mansion, a handsome residence in that city. In 1755 he aided in an effort to raise funds, after Braddock's defeat, and in the following year became a member of the Independent Troop of Horse of Philadelphia. He was a signer of the Non-Importation Agreement of 1765, but subsequently turned loyalist, became the king's agent, and later, like his sister, Phila, removed to England. There he remained for some time after the Revolution, when he returned to Philadelphia, where he resided until his death in 1793. It is very probable that such a prominent man as David Franks had his portrait painted again in later life. His distinguished progeny should not pass without notice, for among their descendants are people whose names are well-known in American life.

A daughter, Abigail, born in 1744, married Andrew Hamilton, January 6, 1768. He was at one time Attorney-General of the State of Pennsylvania, and the grandson of the Andrew Hamilton whose able and brilliant defence of the liberty of the press, in the John Peter Zenger trial in New York, made proverbial the ability of the Philadelphia lawyer. Although the Hamilton name has disappeared from Philadelphia life, the family is still represented by the descendants of Mrs. James Lyle, David Franks' granddaughter, under the names of Morris, Kuhn, Evans, and Mahan in America, and in England by Becketts, Bruces, and Whichotes.[1]

Mary ("Polly") Franks, the second daughter of David Franks, was born in 1748, and died in 1774, in the prime of her life. She was buried in the Christ Church burying ground, in Philadelphia.

Rebecca Franks, another daughter, born in 1758, was a most brilliant woman, and her literary ability and great charm and wit made her one of the shining lights in the brilliant salons of Colonial Philadelphia. Her career has been ably sketched by Mrs. E. F. Ellet, in her "Women of the Revolution," and by Anne Hollingsworth Wharton, in "Through Colonial Doorways."

Of Rebecca Franks, Miss Wharton says: "She was a reigning belle during the British occupation of Philadelphia, when General Howe was in the habit of tying his horse before David Franks' house and going in to have a chat with the ladies and possibly to

1. See Anne Hollingsworth Wharton, in "Salons Colonial and Republican."

enjoy a laugh at some of Miss Rebecca's spirited sallies. Although the beautiful Jewess shared the honors of belledom with fair Willings and Shippens, no one seems to have disputed her title to be considered the wit of her day among womankind."

She was one of the Queens of Beauty at the Meschianza, a splendid fête, given in honor of General Howe before leaving Philadelphia in 1778, and arranged by the ill-fated Major André. Like so many of the Colonial aristocracy, she took the king's side in the Revolutionary struggle. Her grandfather had been the British king's sole agent for the Northern colonies, and her father was the king's agent for Pennsylvania. She married Lieutenant-Colonel Henry Johnson, the British officer who was surprised by Wayne at Stony Point. They later removed to Bath, England, where her husband inherited his father's estate and baronetcy, and attained the rank of General. Many distinguished Americans visited Rebecca Franks there, among them General Winfield Scott, who wrote about her in his autobiography. She died in 1823, and her descendants today are English peers. A handsome portrait has been painted of her by an English artist, and is reproduced in a very interesting pamphlet on "The Jewish Woman in America," by Leon Huhner, A.M., LL.B., who has devoted much time to early American Jewish research.

David Franks also had two sons, Moses and Jacob, both living in England in 1781.

The Levy family, connected with the Franks family through marriage, is also represented in the collection of the Hon. N. Taylor Phillips. Here is a portrait of Moses Levy, the great-grandfather of Rebecca Franks.

He is shown in a full-length and life-size portrait turned to his left and facing front. He wears a red collarless coat and white wig. A muslin neckcloth is folded under his double chin, and the white puffs of his undersleeves show at his wrists. His right hand rests on a table, draped in blue, and his left hand, carried down by his side, is held out with the thumb and index finger well extended. There is a patriarchal dignity about him, with his florid complexion, bold yet regular features, and high forehead. At his feet rests his dog, and in the background is seen a sailing vessel calmly adrift on the deep, with clouds and sky above.

Moses Levy, the son of Isaac Levy, came to New York from England about 1695.[1] He was married twice, his first wife being Rycha Ascher, and his second wife Grace Mears. He died in New York, June 14, 1728. Thomas Sully, as we shall see later, painted a number of portraits of the descendants of this family, several of which are in the possession of Mrs. Robert Hale Bancroft, of Boston.

From the general treatment of painting, it is not unlikely that Moses Levy's portrait and that of Jacob Franks were painted by the same artist. However, all of these unattributed portraits, of the Franks and Levy families, according to Mr. Lawrence Park, were painted by Dutch artists in New York. Pieter Vanderlyn was painting pictures there at that time, and it is possible that some of these were painted by him. Another remote possibility is that they were painted by Jacobus Gerritsen Strycker.

A portrait in the Phillips collection attributed to John Wollaston by Mr. Lawrence Park is that of Rachel Levy, another daughter of Moses Levy. Rachel was the grandmother of Mr. Phillips'

1. Although tradition ascribes Moses Levy's birthplace to Spain, this is doubtless incorrect. It is much more probable that the family originally moved to London from Germany or Holland.

grandmother. She is represented in a life-size painting to the waist, turned to her right and facing the spectator. She wears an exquisite ivory-white satin gown. The tight-fitting bodice is trimmed with wide lace, very delicately rendered. The short sleeves with bands of satin at the elbow are finished with wide white lace. Her dark hair, over which a dainty lace cap is worn, is brushed back from her forehead and worn low at the neck. Her portrait, Mr. Phillips says, has often been greatly admired for its beauty.

This painting, so long unattributed before Mr. Lawrence Park ascribed it to John Wollaston, is of special interest, for Wollaston's portraits, considered good in their time (it has been said that they were painted with a "very pretty taste") still merit considerable praise. Wollaston came from England to visit the colonies about 1772 and painted chiefly in Virginia and Maryland, where many of his paintings can be seen today proudly displayed in the homes of the descendants of the early settlers.

Rachel married Isaac Mendes Seixas, who was born in Lisbon, Portugal, in 1708. He arrived in New York City about the year 1730, when he entered into business. He went with his family to Newport, Rhode Island, about 1765, and resided there until his death, November 3, 1780. Rachel removed to New York City some time after her husband's death, where she died May 12, 1797.

One of her sons, Moses, married Jochabed, daughter of Benjamin and Judith Levy of Newport, Rhode Island, October 3, 1770. Moses was the founder of the Bank of Rhode Island. He was a highly respected member of the community of Jews at Newport, and was Grand Master of the Grand Lodge of Masons of the State of Rhode Island. His death occurred at a visit to his son-in-law, Mr. Naphtali Phillips, of New York, of whom there is a portrait by James Herring in the Phillips collection. After Moses Seixas' death, the bank, which was in his house, continued to stand there until 1818, when it was moved. The Seixas house was afterwards occupied by Commodore Oliver H. Perry, hero of the battle of Lake Erie.

Gershom Mendes Seixas, another of Rachel Levy's sons, was born in New York, January 14, 1745, where he married Miss Elkaly Cohen, September 6, 1775. He evinced a disposition for services in the synagogue, and from 1780–1784 was Minister of the Mikve Israel Synagogue in Philadelphia. When he returned to New York, he served as trustee of Columbia College from 1787–1815. Gershom was a serious and ardent patriot, and in 1789 participated with thirteen other clergymen in the inauguration of President Washington.

There is a reproduction from a bas-relief, by an unknown artist, of Gershom Mendes Seixas, in a very interesting historical sketch of the Congregation Mikve Israel by Dr. A. S. W. Rosenbach.

Benjamin Mendes Seixas, the third son of Rachel and Isaac Seixas, married Zipporah Levy, daughter of Mr. Hayman Levy. Her portrait by an unknown artist is also in the Phillips collection.

The Franks and Levy families cover a period of over two hundred years. No names in American Jewish history are more influential or important. A great number of the present Congregation of the Shearith Israel in New York trace their ancestorship to these distinguished families, and the majority of the worshippers of the Mikve Israel Synagogue in Philadelphia are also descended from these families. Much credit for the facts surrounding the lives of these notable families and for the preservation of their portraits is due to the Hon. N. Taylor Phillips.

There has often been expressed a doubt as to the possibility of giving authentic attribution to these early American portraits. It is, however, from this very search for identifications that a great deal of the pleasure and fascination associated with them is derived. Generally a few well-known methods are employed for making scientific attributions. Primarily, of course, a good portrait reproduces the features, the essential characteristics, and conveys something of the personality of the sitter. Within this general definition, however, may be included infinite variations, due not only to the idiosyncrasies of the sitter, but to the limitations and personality of the artist. It is, of course, the aim of every artist to make his portrait not only interesting to look upon, but true to reality, producing with fidelity such salient traits as the nose, mouth, chin, and eyes. The more subtle features, however, the curl of the hair, a turn to the eye, a finger, the contour of the hand, the drapery, color, atmosphere, studio property, often escape the eye of the layman, but constitute for the student the indices by which artists reveal their own identity.

Thus many an artist hitherto unknown has been revealed by a predilection for some special trait which he imparts to all his work, consciously or because he cannot paint in any other way. The Stuart flesh tints, the gorgeous tactile values of Copley, the almond-eyed beauties of Wollaston are recognized at once. When the trained eye knows these subtleties from constant association with a number of portraits by the same artist, the authorship of a portrait comes sometimes in a flash—unthinkingly.

Among the unattributed paintings of this early period is a portrait of Rabbi Karigal, 1733–1778, the friend of Ezra Stiles, 1727–1795, President of Yale College. The picture is owned by a great-grandson of President Stiles, Mr. MacGregor Jenkins, of Boston. The Rabbi taught Doctor Stiles Hebrew and Sanscrit in exchange for lessons in English, and according to Mr. Jenkins there is a tradition that he came to this country at the invitation of Ezra Stiles. Abiel Holmes' "Life of Ezra Stiles," published in 1789, refers to the friendship and intimacy which existed between the two men. Doctor Stiles, we learn, frequently attended worship at the Newport synagogue where Karigal preached, and was very curious to know the history of this picturesque group whose descendants were already imprinting their culture in this new country.

A photograph hardly does justice to this beautiful old portrait of a Rabbi with his left hand holding a book, and his right hand pointing upwards with admonitory finger, which Mr. Jenkins said often hushed the children of his household into silence and obedience. From under his high fur turban the Rabbi looks at us with an air of wise benevolence and with an unmistakable gleam of Jewish wit. He wears an outer garment of deep red or terra cotta, and a white cravat. His beard is long and black and his upper lip partly shaven. The upper right hand corner of the canvas bears this inscription:

> *Rabbi Raphael Haijm Karigal*
> *Born at Hebron, educated there and at Jerusalem and died*
> *at Barcelona*
> *Aetat*
> *MDCCLXII 1772*

When Mr. Jenkins gave me the Karigal photograph, he also gave me a copy of the Stiles portrait, which is assumed to have been given in exchange for that of the Rabbi, and expressed the hope that a study of the technique of these portraits would reveal their authorship. The technique of the two pictures is quite at variance, and the Karigal portrait is still unattributed, but shortly after my conversation with Mr. Jenkins, in reading the diary of Ezra Stiles, I came upon the following passage dated August 1, 1771, which gives the attribution of the Stiles portrait to Samuel King:

Mr. King finished my picture. He began it last year, but went over the face again now and added Emblems, etc. The pice is made up thus. The effigy is in a green elbow chair in a teaching attitude, with the right hand on the breast and the left holding a teaching Bible. Behind and on the left side is a part of a library, two shelves of books. A folio with Latin and Hebrew works, also the History of China. By these I denote my taste for history. At my right hand stands a pillar. These emblems are more descriptive of my mind than the effigies of my face.

Among the many portraits of past Grand Masters of Masonry hanging in the large assembly hall of the Boston Masonic Temple is that of a handsome middle-aged gray-haired gentleman. It is the portrait of the father of Judah Hays, Moses Michael Hays, who was born in New York in 1738. He settled in Newport and established himself later in business in Boston, where he died May 9, 1805. *The Columbian Centinel*, published in Boston at that time, contained the following typical eighteenth century obituary:

In the character of the deceased there is much worthy of our admiration, much for our imitation. Possessed by nature of a strong intellect, there was a vigor in his conceptions of men and things which gave a seeming asperity to his conversation, which was ever frank and lucid. He walked abroad fearing no man, but loving all. Under his roof dwelt hospitality; it was an asylum of friendship, the mansion of peace. He was without guile, despising hypocrisy, as he despised meanness. Take him for all in all, he was a Man.

The portrait, which is a copy from the original, still remains unattributed.

Another unattributed portrait is that of Israel Jacobs, 1714–1810, which shows a very interesting head with a rather striking resemblance to Benjamin Franklin. Jacobs was a member of the Pennsylvania Assembly in 1771, and of the United States Congress, 1791–1793. Despite his high political connections, he was a man of rather ordinary attainments by comparison with his wife, Zippora Nunez Machado, who was a woman of great beauty and a linguist among other accomplishments. Her first husband was the Rev. David Mendes Machado. There is a portrait of a daughter by her first marriage, Rebecca Machado, the wife of Jonas Phillips. Mrs. Phillips' portrait, life-size, is painted in a sitting position with her shapely arms resting lightly on her lap. A black lace scarf is worn over her bodice, which is filled in at the neck with folds of white muslin, and short black curls are clustered in regular fashion under her smart lace cap.

The portrait of her husband, Jonas Phillips, shows an aristocratic white-haired man of portly mien, wearing a collared brown coat, a buff waistcoat, a white stock collar, with bow, and a ruffled shirt. These portraits of Jonas Phillips and his wife have been attributed by Mr. Frank W. Bayley to Charles Willson Peale, who was born in Maryland in 1741. In 1768 he studied with Benjamin West in London, and on his return established himself in Philadelphia. In 1772 he painted, at Mount Vernon, the earliest portrait of Washington in existence. According to his son, Rembrandt, he painted fourteen portraits of Washington from life. Charles

Willson Peale died in Philadelphia, February 22, 1827. The portrait of Jonas Phillips and a copy of his wife's portrait are in the possession of the American Jewish Historical Society, while the original portrait of Mrs. Phillips is in the possession of Mr. Isaac Graff of New York.

Phillips, the first of his distinguished family to settle in America, came from Germany, where he was born in 1736. Among other things he was a signer in 1770 of resolutions relating to Non-Importation, was in the Revolutionary Army, and was a founder of the Mikve Israel Congregation in Philadelphia. He died in that city, January 29, 1803. His widow survived until 1831, and among their numerous progeny of twenty-one children, a number achieved great prominence as lawyers, actors, playwrights, and journalists. A daughter, Rachel Phillips, was the mother of Commodore Uriah P. Levy, who brought about the abolition of corporal punishment in the United States Navy.

Uriah P. Levy was born in Philadelphia, April 22, 1792. Promoted from cabin boy to the rank of Commodore, he was, at the time of his death in 1862, the highest ranking officer in the United States Navy. He served in the War of 1812, and in recognition of his valuable services to the nation was voted the freedom of the city of New York. Levy was a great admirer of Thomas Jefferson, and the famous bronze statue of the latter, in the Capitol at Washington, modelled by David d'Angers, the French sculptor, is the gift of Levy to the United States Government. This was a unique gift, as all other works of art in the possession of the government had been paid for by Congress or State Legislatures. The beautifully wrought sculpture, symbolizing American liberty, represents Jefferson as just having signed the Declaration of Independence. Nor was this the only instance in which Levy showed his appreciation of Jefferson. When Jefferson died, Levy purchased his large estate in Monticello, Virginia. The erection of this estate began in 1764. The road still leads up grade to Monticello all the way from Charlottesville. Here was hauled the timber to be fashioned on the spot; the nails were wrought in a forge constructed nearby, and artisans came from Europe to supervise operations. The result was an imposing structure surmounted by a dome. Within were spacious rooms with floors inlaid of satinwood and rosewood. Especially beautiful was the living room, with its open fireplace, and balustraded gallery, which has often been praised in superlative terms. This historic home Commodore Levy left, upon his death, in March, 1862, to the people of the United States for the maintenance of an agricultural school for the children of deceased warrant-officers of the United States Navy. The legality of the bequest was disputed, and the property reverted to Levy's heirs.

However, Commodore Levy's original wish that Monticello remain a national shrine has been fulfilled. Within recent years the Thomas Jefferson Memorial Foundation purchased the mansion from Jefferson M. Levy, owner of the estate, and restored it to almost the precise condition as when occupied by Jefferson.

Uriah P. Levy's portrait still rightfully hangs in Monticello, where it has been for over fifty years. I am indebted to Mr. Theodore Fred Kuper, of the Thomas Jefferson Memorial Foundation, for the photograph of this splendid portrait. Mr. Frank W. Bayley attributes the portrait to Thomas Buchanan Read, 1822–1872, famous for his painting of "Sheridan's Ride," and for the many portraits he painted of men who fought in the War of 1812 and in the Mexican War.

Charles Willson Peale, who, it is supposed, painted the portraits of Mr. and Mrs. Jonas Phillips, imparted the gift for art to his sons. In the work of Rembrandt, the second son, is the portrait of Judge Moses Levy, who was born in Philadelphia in 1758. He was the son of Samson Levy, an ardent patriot and signer of the Non-Importation Agreement in 1765. Moses Levy entered the University of Pennsylvania in 1772, and was admitted to the Bar in Philadelphia in 1778. He was Recorder of Philadelphia from 1802–1822. In 1822 he became Presiding Judge of the District Court of Philadelphia, in which office he continued until 1825. It is probable that it was he who had been considered by Jefferson for the office of Attorney-General of the United States. Levy also had the distinction of being one of the trustees of the University of Pennsylvania, from 1802 to the time of his death in 1826. He married Mary Pearce, 1763–1850, whose portrait, also painted by Rembrandt Peale, hangs with his own in the home of his great-grandson, Mr. J. J. Milligan of Baltimore.

Levy's portrait shows him in a sitting position with his left arm resting on his chair. He wears a dark blue coat and ruffled shirt, which, with his silvery colored hair, is in pleasing contrast to his dark brown eyes. The background, revealing a curtain, is in tones of brown. Mrs. Levy, dressed in black satin, wears a white lace veil over her powdered hair, long loose white gloves, and a kerchief about her neck. A large brown turkey-feathered fan, held in her hand, quaintly decorates the portrait.

The Peale family ranks with the foremost in its contributions to portraiture in this country. Rembrandt Peale's fame rests on his portrait of Washington, which he painted at the age of seventeen. He then went to England to study under Benjamin West and, when he returned, painted portraits in New York, Philadelphia, and the South. Subsequently he went to Italy, taking with him his portrait of Washington, which brought him great distinction. He was President of the American Academy, in succession to Trumbull, and was one of the charter members of the National Academy of Design. He died in Philadelphia, October 3, 1860.

When I received the portraits of Mr. and Mrs. Israel Israel, from Mr. Arthur G. Ellet, of Kansas City, the late Lawrence Park had already passed away, and I was, therefore, unable to avail myself of his expert opinion as to the identity of the artists who painted these two portraits. Both are life-size and in oil. The Israel Israels were also prominent in Philadelphia.

Mr. Israel is represented well advanced in years, in a sitting position, wearing a dark blue coat and holding a document dated 1793 in his left hand. Particularly noticeable are the large brown eyes, the drooping lids, the shaggy eyebrows, the right one being slightly arched, and the gray silky hair which surmounts his well-modelled, markedly Jewish features.

Family tradition, according to Mr. Ellet, attributes the portrait to Benjamin West. While traditions are interesting, they are not wholly reliable. Benjamin West could hardly have painted this portrait, because there are no resemblances to his mannerisms. Besides, West was born in 1753, and at the age of twenty-one, in 1774, embarked for Europe, and never returned. Mr. Israel was born in 1743, and at the date of West's sailing was only thirty-one years of age. As the picture portrays Israel in his late maturity, it seems conclusive enough that the painting must have been made by some other artist. It is a very good portrait, however, and it is hoped that the future will reveal its authorship.

The portrait of Mrs. Israel (Hannah Erwin), obviously painted by another artist, also remains without attribution. She is pictured in a sitting position, holding a book in her right hand and facing the spectator. A decorative scarf and dainty muslin cap offset the Quaker-like simplicity of her dress, and her clear blue eyes and brown hair relieve the austerity of her expression.

The Israels are also represented in two very lovely pastels, rich and delicate in coloring, which hang, with their original frames, in the home of Mrs. James Alden Valentine, of East Walpole, Massachusetts. These portraits, also unattributed, portray the Israels in their earlier years.

Mrs. Valentine is the great-granddaughter of Israel Israel, and from her and her very gracious mother, Mrs. Elvira Augusta Ellet Kendall, I gathered information about the Israels hitherto unpublished.

Mrs. Israel was born in Wilmington, Delaware, of a Quaker family. Israel Israel, a native of Pennsylvania, was the son of Michael Israel, a Jew, and Mary J. Paxton, a member of the Episcopal Church.

When Israel Israel was twenty-one years old, he left America for the Barbadoes and, within ten years, amassed a considerable fortune and returned to his native country, where he married Miss Erwin in 1775. Mrs. Valentine showed me the marriage certificate, which was carefully wrapped with a portion of a very old parchment scroll of the Book of Esther written in Hebrew.

The patriotism of the Israels during the Revolution, their hardships and heroic deeds are interestingly recorded in Elizabeth F. Ellet's "Women of the Revolution."

In 1800 Mr. Israel became High-Sheriff of Philadelphia, which office he held for three years, and was also Grand Master of the Masonic Order in Pennsylvania in 1802 and in 1804. Another portrait of Israel Israel hangs in the Grand Master's Room in the Masonic Temple in Philadelphia. He died in 1821. Mrs. Israel passed away at the age of fifty-six at their country place near Philadelphia in 1813.

They reared a large and prominent family. Their daughter, Mary, married Charles Ellet, and from this union sprang the great Ellet family of the Mississippi Ram Fleet and Marine Brigade, which attained fame during the Civil War. Charles Ellet, Jr., their son, was particularly well-known for his daring engineering feats. His daughter, Mary Virginia Ellet, who is now Mrs. Cabell, was for a great many years President Presiding of the Daughters of the American Revolution. She is a cousin of ex-Secretary of the Navy Josephus Daniels and of U. S. Senator John Daniels of Virginia.

Mrs. Valentine has inherited a number of valuable things from the Israel Israel home. Among them, a large set of Royal Sèvres china, some old dinner knives of Damascus steel, an I. Anthony coffee pot, and a number of solid silver pieces, including tea pots, a creamer, and a beautiful bowl, marked "F. W." She also owns three of the silver coat buttons worn by Israel Israel, and the black lace shawl which Mrs. Israel wears in the pastel painting. A most unusual piece of furniture from the Israel family finds its resting place in Mrs. Valentine's home. It is a mahogany sewing table, easily converted into a writing desk, with two pockets, one on each side, and supported by white mahogany spindles alternating with black. Mr. Israel gave a handsome clock to his wife in 1775, which Mary, the daughter, inherited, and which was later presented by her to the Historical Society of Pennsylvania.

Of all the mementos that came down to Mrs. Valentine from Israel Israel, the most notable and most interesting was a letter written by the Reverend Henry Muhlenberg to Mr. Israel, dated March 31, 1784.

This letter, written in the quaint bold script of that day, and of which I made an exact copy, reads as follows:

DEAR MR. ISRAEL

I received your Favor by the Rev^d Mr. Wade and complying with your Request, found in our Church Records, that by Holy Baptism you were adopted and made a child of God and an Inheritor of the Kingdom of Heaven, on the 13th Day of June Anno Domini 1746; done upon serious Petitioning of your tender loving Mother, on whose Breast you lay yet and were about a year old. Your Father professed to be a Jew outwardly and your Mother a well meaning Christian and Member of the English Church. She lived in Friendship with several families of the English Church in the Townships of Newhannover, Oly, etc: where John Campbell Esq., William Mangridge Esq., Edward Drury A;. and their respective Families in them Times kept up an edifying Society and used the Means of Grace for Salvation.

Accordingly on the said 13th Day of June 1746 you were dedicated unto Jehova, the Most Adorable Father, Son and Holy Ghost, by your beloved Mother, by me and Madam Mary Campbell in the Presence of several Evidences. The Covenant was performed by Prayers, Promise and Vow, that you, dear Israel, when living and arriving to years of Discretion, should be instructed to renew the Solemn Promise and Vow, which was made in your Name, should ratify and confirm the same in your own Person and acknowledge yourself bound by the Grace of God and your serious Endeavours, to know, to believe and to do all, whatsover is revealed in the Old and New Testament of the Holy Bible and extracted out of the same and set forth in the Catechism of the Church, as most necessary to Eternal Salvation. Madam Campbell has departed this life and been called home many years ago; and your Absence from me, has not permitted to enquire, whether you have performed the solemn Promise and Vow? not knowing whether you were alive or dead. But I hope your dear mother has remember'd and affectionately exhorted you to observe your Duty. But in Case you had neglected Instruction and gone astray like a lost Sheep in the Wilderness, then I beseech you, for God's Sake to lay hold on the Means of Grace in Order to be led by the Operations and Influence of the Holy Spirit into true Repentance, living Faith and Godliness. And since you have an Opportunity to be instructed in the Way of Salvation by the Rev^d Mr. Wade, then improve the Time and Opportunity and follow the example of Truly approved Christians, in as much as they follow our ever blessed Saviour and walk in his Commandments. Which is the fervent Prayer of Dear Mr. Israel, your well wishing a: dying Friend: Henry Muhlenberg Senr.

New Providence
March: 31st 1784.

In contrast to Israel Israel's father, who outwardly professed Judaism, was his mother, "a well-meaning Christian," who, according to the good Reverend, was extremely anxious that the infant be "made a child of God and an inheritor of the Kingdom of Heaven"—by baptism. The pious minister was no less solicitous that Israel earn eternal salvation—by confirming the baptism and by believing and doing all that is revealed in the Old and New Testament. Thus one more Jewish soul is to be saved from eternal perdition.

In the collection of Mr. J. Bunford Samuel, of Philadelphia, is a portrait of Rachel Levy, the wife of Aaron Levy. It is said that Rachel was a redemptionist and that one day Aaron, seeing her in tears, like Ruth "amid the alien corn," while at work on the Sabbath on the steps of the Chew House in Philadelphia, took compassion on her, married her, and gave her the education then considered suitable for a young woman of her position. She is represented in a slightly less than life-size portrait sitting in a red chair. Over the shoulders and neck of her tightly-fitting bodice are soft fluffy folds of white muslin, and around her plump throat is a string of yellow beads. Her white scant cap is topped with a cluster of blue ribbons.

Her husband, Aaron Levy, is also represented in portraiture. Dr. A. S. W. Rosenbach owns a miniature painting of him, and there is a life-size portrait of Aaron in the possession of the Clay family in Lexington, Kentucky. Aaron Levy, born in 1742, was a wealthy landowner of his day. In 1779 he purchased a large tract of land in Center County, Pennsylvania, and called it "Aaronsville." Hoping some day that it would become the capital of the state, he laid out a town of pretentious proportions. Except on paper, the town never realized its founder's dreams. However, the village, as it now stands, consists largely of a magnificent street flanked on either side by charming houses of the Colonial period, which give it a quiet dignity. As Aaron advanced in years he became "land poor," and when the Gratz family assured him a comfortable annuity, he relinquished claim to his Philadelphia property, in their favor, and retired to Aaronsville. His Philadelphia property, located at Spring Hill and Garden Streets, incomparably valuable today, formed a large share in the basis of the Gratz wealth.

Another portrait in Mr. Samuel's collection is a quaint silhouette of his grandfather, John Moss, who was born in London in 1771, and died in Philadelphia in 1847. Mr. Samuel recently purchased two white marble lions, weighing two tons each, which had been placed as an ornament on the steps of the old Merchants' Exchange in Philadelphia by Mr. Moss one hundred years ago. As the Exchange was being rebuilt, it was decided to relegate the lions to the scrap heap, and on this disclosure Mr. Samuel purchased back his grandfather's lions and took them to his summer home at Sea Girt. Mr. Moss was the first to ship abroad a load of Pennsylvania anthracite coal, in return for which he obtained a highly remunerative cargo of bandanna handkerchiefs. He was a director in several railroad companies, was interested in Masonry, and was one of the committee on the Damascus episode, which marked the first concerted action since the Fall of Jerusalem on the part of Jews all over the world in behalf of their less fortunate brothers. The authorship of the silhouette was unknown until quite recently, when it was attributed by Mrs. Ethel Stanwood Bolton to William Henry Brown.

Brown, known as the "last of the silhouettists," was born in 1808 in Charleston, South Carolina, of Quaker ancestry. Showing an inclination for his work at an early age, he soon became noted in his own day, and shared with Edouart the honors of a master craftsman in his field. Brown cut the whole figure very rapidly— his time varying from one to five minutes. During his lifetime he made many portraits of distinguished contemporaries; among them were Chief Justice John Marshall, John Quincy Adams, Andrew Jackson, John C. Calhoun, and others, all of which are reproduced in Brown's own book, "Portrait Gallery of Distinguished Citizens with Biographical Sketches."

Other portraits in Philadelphia of high artistic worth are in the possession of Dr. I. Minis Hays and merit consideration. Among the most interesting are two beautiful portraits of Mr. and Mrs. Manuel Josephson, by Jeremiah Theus.

An unusually fine portrait is this likeness of Manuel Josephson, life-size to the waist and turned toward his left, with his eyes facing front. He wears a gray suit trimmed with a collar and large buttons. A white neckcloth tied under his chin is tucked into his high buttoned waistcoat. His right arm rests by his side, and his left hand, showing exquisite lace at his wrist, is thrust into his waistcoat. Markedly beautiful is the oval face with its high forehead, long but shapely nose, and well-formed mouth and chin. Manuel Josephson was born in 1729. During the years 1785–1791 he was president of the Mikve Israel Congregation in Philadelphia. He married Ritzel Judah.

Mrs. Josephson is portrayed in a life-size portrait to the waist, turned slightly towards her right, with her luminous eyes front. Her tight-fitting blue satin bodice in décolletage is trimmed with lace cleverly rendered. Ruffled sleeves also disclose lace just above the wrists, and a dainty lace collar encircles her throat. On her dark brown hair, brushed back from a high forehead, is a red rose.

The love for sheeny satins, colorful waistcoats, and attractive accessories; in fact, the general gayety of apparel so apparent in the dress of our early Americans is effectively brought out in these paintings by Jeremiah Theus, who, when he died in 1774, amassed a comfortable fortune from his painting.

Theus was born in Switzerland, and came about 1739 with two brothers to South Carolina. His work was chiefly confined to the South, where the following notice appeared in the *Gazette* of Charleston, South Carolina, August 30, 1740:

Jeremiah Theus, Limner, gives notice that he is removed into Market Square, near John Laurens, Sadler, where all Gentlemen and Ladies may have their pictures drawn, likewise Landscapes of all sizes. Crests and Coats of Arms for Coaches or Chaises. Likewise for the convenience of those who live in the country he is willing to wait on them at their respective plantations.

There is hardly a southern family of note and position which is not represented in the canvases of this versatile artist.

In Doctor Hays' collection there is also a portrait of Barnard Gratz, 1738–1801 (brother of Michael Gratz), and one of his wife, Richea Meyers, 1731–1801, who was the daughter of Sampson Meyers.[1] Barnard is seated at a table with spectacles in his right hand against a background of drapery and books. He came to Philadelphia from Germany when about seventeen years of age and entered into a partnership with Michael, trading with the Indians, and supplying the government with Indian goods. He was one of the signers of the Non-Importation Resolution and was a trustee of the Mikve Israel Congregation, Philadelphia. Charles Peale Polk, who painted the portrait, was a nephew of the noted artist Charles Willson Peale, and is celebrated for having painted some fifty portraits of Washington from memory.

The portrait of Richea Gratz in which she wears a red dress cut low about her lovely neck, has been attributed by Lawrence Park to Robert Feke, the early Newport painter, who was receiving commissions in Philadelphia at this time.

With this collection also hangs a most interesting pastel by James Sharples of Samuel Hays, the grandfather of Doctor Hays. Samuel Hays, 1764–1839, lived in Philadelphia, where he was engaged in the East India trade and married Richea Gratz, daugh-

1. Or Mears.

ter of Mr. and Mrs. Michael Gratz. This Sharples pastel exhibits those qualities of grace and charm found in the large collection in the Old State House, in Philadelphia, where there is an array of the notabilities of his day to whom in his sojourns he made requests for portraits. In this manner, travelling about as an itinerant artist in a four-wheeled carriage of his own contrivance, and carrying with him his wife and three children and all his implements, Sharples accumulated a considerable fortune, although his charges were only fifteen dollars for a profile and twenty dollars for a full face.

Other Philadelphians prominent in the days of the Revolution, were Mr. and Mrs. Joseph Andrews, son-in-law and daughter of Haym Salomon, who rendered important services to the cause of the Revolution. Sallie Andrews, 1779–1854, was reputed to have been a great coquette in her youth, and of fair complexion, dark hazel eyes, and brown hair. She was active in social and philanthropic work in Philadelphia, where she was born during the Revolution, and died in New York City at the age of seventy-four. One of her seventeen children, Joseph I. Andrews, married Miriam Nones of New York, the daughter of Major Benjamin Nones of Revolutionary fame, and the daughter of this union is Mrs. E. L. Goldbaum, of Memphis, Tennessee, the owner of the original portraits of the Andrews.[1]

Mrs. Andrews wears, in the portrait, an oriental head-dress, ivory in color, with lavender shadows. About her dark wisteria dress is a white lace kerchief. Her jewels of pearls and diamonds are now in the possession of her great-great-grandchild, Joseph Franklin Andrews, of Memphis. Mr. Joseph Andrews, her hus-

1. Letters from Mrs. E. L. Goldbaum.

band, was born in New York City and died in Philadelphia. At the time the portrait was painted, he was a retired banker. His suit is of dark cloth, his vest of tan cloth. He is seated in a dark red chair and holds his Bible and spectacles in hand. Like his wife, he was also of fair complexion with hazel eyes and luxuriant dark hair.[1]

An artist to whom recognition is now being accorded in greater measure was John Wesley Jarvis, who was born in England in 1780, and came to this country at a very early age. He was chiefly self-taught, and received some instruction in the painting of miniatures from Malbone. Many of his portraits can be found in the New York City Hall, in eastern municipal halls, and in old southern manors. Henry Inman, who was a pupil, often painted in backgrounds and draperies under the master's directions. A distinguished example of Jarvis' work, now owned by Professor Samuel Mordecai, of Durham, North Carolina, is the portrait of Jacob Mordecai, who, in September, 1774, as a young sergeant, escorted into Philadelphia the first American Congress. At the age of twenty-three, he married Judith Myers of New York, and at her death married Rebecca, a half-sister of his wife. He settled in Warrenton, North Carolina, about 1787, where he established a Seminary for Young Ladies, which brought him no little fame. Jarvis seems to rise above the commonplace in this picture in revealing the character of his sitter, with his fine silvery head, gentle mouth, and thoughtful eyebrows.

Another Jarvis portrait is that of Mordecai M. Noah, the great American Jewish liberator and nationalist, who was born in Philadelphia, July 19, 1785. He was a conspicuous figure as editor and

1. Letters from Mrs. E. L. Goldbaum.

publisher of several newspapers, and as consul in Tunis. Impressed with the unfortunate condition of the Jews in Europe, he purchased in 1825, on his return, twenty-five hundred acres of land at Grand Island, New York, which he called "Ararat," and issued a manifesto for Jews to migrate there. The plan did not materialize, but he never relinquished the hope of the ultimate restoration of the Jews to Palestine. The portrait is now owned by Mr. Robert L. Noah, of New York City.

Another fine portrait by Jarvis is that of Major Mordecai Myers. He was born in Newport, Rhode Island, in 1776 and died in Schenectady in 1870, full of years and honor. His father was a friend of Dr. Ezra Stiles. As a youth he studied military tactics with Colonel de la Croix, a French officer who had served under Napoleon. His military experiences are recorded in "Reminiscences, 1812–14, by Major M. Myers, 13th Infantry, U. S Army." His sword is in the National Museum in Washington, D. C. Myers was in the Battle of Crysler's Field on the Niagara Frontier, and was taken wounded to the house of Doctor Mann, where he remained four months. Here he met Miss Charlotte Bailey, who became his wife. They resided at Kinderhook, near Albany, where Myers was president of the village, and where he publicly received and addressed Martin Van Buren on his return home at the end of his term as President of the United States. He was an enthusiastic Freemason, and was elected six times to the New York State Assembly. Myers, with his low, cultured voice and charming manner, was a splendid host, and in his circle of friends whom he was delighted to see and entertain were Aaron Burr, De Witt Clinton, and Alexander Hamilton. Myers' oldest daughter, Henrietta, married Peter S. Hoes, nephew of ex-President Van Buren. A son, Theodorus Bailey Myers, was Lieutenant-Commander of the United States Navy, and had a magnificent library at his home at Four West Thirty-fourth Street, now the Waldorf Astoria Hotel. The lives of Myers' distinguished family are recorded in a privately circulated volume, "Biographical Sketches of the Bailey-Myers-Mason Families, 1776–1905." Two portraits of him are known to be extant. One, a miniature by Tisdale, painted in 1799, depicts a young man whose wistful aspect belies his twenty-two years. In the Jarvis portrait painted in January, 1810, when he was thirty-three, he wears the uniform of the United States Army. His fine eyes and expressive features are well defined in this notable Jarvis painting.

In the Maryland Historical Society are two interesting Jarvis portraits. One is of Mrs. Solomon Etting, née Rachel Gratz, the daughter of Barnard Gratz, and first cousin of Rebecca and Rachel Gratz. She was born in 1764 and died in 1831. The portrait presents an animated woman of middle age, with olive complexion, dark eyes, and dark brown hair. She wears a lace cap with streamers tied in bow fashion about a moderately plump neck, over which is a small white veil fastened with a handsome brooch. A lace shawl of delicate texture, almost Copley-like in its feathery detail, adorns her portly shoulders. The painting falls short of the elegance of a Stuart, but gives a characterization of a well-defined personality, and reminds one at moments of the smiling matrons of Franz Hals.

A little more austere and philosophical, rather more reflective in disposition, is the portrait of her husband, Solomon Etting, 1764–1847, who was a man of great ability and energy. He anticipated by a generation the efforts of Disraeli and Baron Lionel de Rothschild, in the cause of Jewish emancipation, by making successive petitions to the Legislature of Maryland from 1816–1826, to make it possible for the Jews there to hold public office without first declaring a belief in the Christian religion. There is a subtle harmony of composition and treatment in this portrait which shows him writing at a table, his left hand resting on the arm of his chair. He wears a dark suit and white stock collar cut low under the neck. Particularly appealing are the blue eyes, moderately large, searching, yet kindly.

A survey of early American portraiture of Jewish people in this country would not be complete without some notice of the works of Charles Balthazar Julien Fevret de St. Mémin, born in Dijon, France, March 12, 1770, and for some time a resident in this country. This curious artist, who has left some strangely quaint likenesses of celebrated families in America, made, among others, a drawing of Hyman Marks, which is in the possession of the American Jewish Historical Society, and portraits of Henry Alexander, Solomon Moses, and Abraham Hart.[1] Drawings of Mrs. Samson Levy, Senior (Martha Lampley), and her son, Samson, Junior, are owned by a descendant, Mrs. Robert Hale Bancroft, of Boston, and an engraving of the wife of Samson, Junior, who was Sarah Coates, reduced from the original St. Mémin portrait, is in the possession of Mrs. Albert Bache, Philadelphia. St. Mémin's method of portraiture was unique. He first made a life-sized portrait with black crayon on pink paper, by the aid of a mechanical device of his own invention which he called a "phy-

1. Dacosta, who has been included in the list of Jewish subjects by St. Mémin, was not a Jew but a Spanish Catholic. His full name was Jose Roiz Da Costa. Isaac Dacosta, the Jew, died about 1784. As St. Mémin was born in 1770 he could hardly have drawn Isaac Dacosta's portrait. From a note by Samuel Oppenheim.

sionotrace," and then reproduced the crayon upon a small copper plate, two inches in diameter. He framed the crayon and gave it with the plate and twelve proofs to his sitter for thirty-three dollars. It is rather interesting to note that a St. Mémin portrait can bring as much as five hundred dollars or more today, depending upon the importance of the subject. A complete set with the name of each subject is at the Corcoran Gallery, Washington, District of Columbia.

II

MINIATURES

A FORM of painting which enjoyed great vogue in Colonial days was the miniature, adorned in frames of simple beauty or richly decorated with precious gems. Great sentiment and romance attached to these dainty intimate treasures, which sometimes enclosed a lock of hair, as they were often lovers' gifts. They were painted on ivory and executed in water colors, the flesh tints and other parts requiring great delicacy of finish, to preserve the freshness of the complexion, and the transparency of blood and vein underneath the skin.

At the observance of the one hundred and twenty-fifth Anniversary of the Inauguration of George Washington, at a meeting of the Daughters and Sons of the American Revolution in New York City, May, 1914, mention was made of the miniature of Colonel David Salisbury Franks and the history of his brilliant career recalled. He served as an American diplomatic agent and officer in the American Revolutionary Army. He was an aide-de-camp to Benedict Arnold, after whose trial for treason he conducted Mrs. Arnold, at the request of Washington, to her home in Philadelphia. In this trial Franks was also implicated but honorably acquitted, and subsequently went to Europe as bearer of despatches to Jay in Madrid and to Franklin in Paris. On his return he was reinstated in the army with rank of Major and was granted four hundred acres of land in recognition of his services during the war. He was one of the original members of the Cincinnati, Pennsylvania Division. The miniature owned by Mrs. Clarence I. De Sola, of Montreal, Canada, was painted in 1776 at Valley Forge, for the sum of seventy-five dollars, by Charles Willson Peale, 1741–1827, one of the finest of the American miniature and portrait painters. It shows an unusually scrupulous attention to detail. The hair is powdered, and the coat is a military blue. It is exquisitely done and encased in its original simple gold frame with glass on both sides.[1]

Mr. Bunford Samuel of Philadelphia owns an unattributed miniature of Jacob De Leon, the known facts of whose life are meagre. There is a tradition, however, that as a captain on General Pulaski's staff, he fought at the Battle of Camden, South Carolina, and with Captain De La Motta and Major Benjamin Nones, carried the mortally wounded De Kalb from the field.[2] The powdered hair, the claret-colored coat with gilt buttons, and the ruffled shirt make a pleasing Colonial portrait.

Miss Eleanor S. Cohen, of Baltimore, has a photograph from the miniature of her maternal great-grandfather, Isaac C. Moses, who died April 3, 1834. The present ownership of the original is unknown to her. There is also in her possession a composite miniature of Kitty Etting Cohen, 1799–1837, the sister of Miriam Etting and the wife of Benjamin I. Cohen. After Mrs. Cohen's death, a son and daughter sat for a miniature which is said to be an excellent likeness.[3]

In the Maryland Historical Society there is a collection of miniatures in the Cohen Room, among which is the still unattributed

1. Letters from Mrs. Clarence I. De Sola, Montreal.
2. Dr. Barnett A. Elzas discredits this tradition in his book on the "Jews of South Carolina."
3. Letters from Miss Eleanor S. Cohen, Baltimore.

miniature of Mrs. Solomon Etting, apparently done when she was Rachel Gratz. The features which Jarvis painted in their maturity are here delineated in a delicate youthful manner. The young woman's light brown hair and fair complexion are set off exquisitely by her white dress. There are also two miniatures here of her distinguished husband attributed to Benjamin Trott. One shows Mr. Etting in profile with the same fine blue eyes and white hair that we see in the Jarvis painting. The other represents a front view, the hair brown, the suit gray, evidently of a more youthful period.

Benjamin Trott was among the formidable rivals of Malbone in his day. He was born probably in Boston about 1770. He painted in New York and Philadelphia, and was a friend of Stuart, whose oils he copied in miniature. When Trott exhibited at the Pennsylvania Academy, it was said that his little paintings had all the force and effect of the best oil pictures. This was the more commendable as Trott was purely an American, and had never come under the influence of foreign study. He would probably have excelled as a painter had he not devoted considerable time in experimenting with devices to convey colors to ivory, but, in the course of these experiments, he discovered some unusually fine pigments which gave his work an exquisite clarity.

A miniature in the Cohen Room, attributed to Trott, of Benjamin I. Cohen, 1797–1845, son of Israel I. Cohen, and son-in-law of Solomon Etting, is singularly sweet and expressive. Against a gray background, the romantic features of this handsome young man in his Byronic ruffles make a striking portrait. Another miniature said to be by Trott is that of Joseph Solomon, the father-in-law of Elijah Etting, the founder of the Etting family in America.

Solomon was born in London in 1700 and died in this country in 1780. The portrait reveals small blue eyes, a gray wig, pale complexion, strongly marked Semitic features, and a mouth and chin feminine to the point of indulgence—comfortable and complacent in his appearance like the Colonial patricians at ease on their plantations.

In the Maryland Historical Society are also miniatures by the greatest of the American miniaturists, Edward Greene Malbone, who was born in Newport in 1777. Among the precious miniatures which he painted in his short career, for he was only thirty years old at the time of his death, is a charming oval of Miriam Etting Myers, 1787–1808, the daughter of Solomon and Rachel Etting, and wife of Jacob Myers. Her brown eyes, fair complexion, and white Empire dress, make a luminous portrait against the delicate blue background.

Even more beautiful are his portraits of the famous Gratz sisters, whom he met through Mr. and Mrs. J. Ogden Hoffman, of New York, at whose home the Gratz girls were frequent visitors. Here they became acquainted with many members of the brilliant circle which gave New York literary distinction in the early years of the nineteenth century—William Cullen Bryant, James Fenimore Cooper, John Inman, brother of Henry Inman, the artist, Henry Tuckerman, and Washington Irving. The latter was engaged to the Hoffmans' daughter, Matilda, to whom Rebecca was devotedly attached, and whom she nursed during her fatal illness. Ever afterward, a beautiful friendship existed between Irving and Miss Gratz, and when he spoke of her subsequently to Walter Scott, the latter was so impressed by the beauty of her character that he immortalized his friend's friend in his conception of

Rebecca in "Ivanhoe."[1] It was from the Hoffman family that Edward Malbone brought letters of introduction to Miss Gratz, from whom he received encouragement and numerous commissions. A miniature of Rachel was presented by him as a gift to Mrs. Hoffman.

Malbone's feeling for beauty and grace gives the exquisite miniatures of the Gratz sisters a sweet and charming purity of expression. These lovely young women, in their dainty Empire frocks of white dotted muslin, had no hesitation to entrust the painting of their portraits to this artist, of whom Washington Allston, a contemporary, said: "No woman ever lost any beauty from his hand." The miniature of Rebecca is owned by Miss Rachel Gratz Nathan, of New York, and that of Rachel is in the possession of Mrs. John Hunter, of Savannah, Georgia.

1. Anne Hollingsworth Wharton, "Heirlooms in Miniatures."

III

THE GREAT AMERICAN MASTERS
GILBERT STUART AND
THOMAS SULLY

AS MALBONE was the greatest of the American miniaturists, so Gilbert Stuart was the greatest of the American
portrait painters. He was born near Newport, Rhode
Island, December 3, 1755. At the age of eighteen, after some
training, he went abroad to study and returned within two years
destitute of everything but the great gift. Before long, however,
the Jews of Newport discovered his genius, and shortly after his
return he began to paint portraits of the wealthy Jewish families
then living there, including the Lopez family, of whose portraits
now, unfortunately, there is no trace.[1] The subjects of a portrait
painter play a part more significant in the development of an
artist than is commonly recognized. Perhaps it is not too much
to infer that through the early recognition of his genius by these
Jews, Stuart's great career was started, receiving that early impetus
which often makes the point of demarcation between an indiffer-
ent success and a career of surpassing distinction. In this sense
Gilbert Stuart and the world owe much to the Jews. In 1775,
Stuart went abroad, again, and after a short career in London,
where he rivalled Reynolds and Gainsborough in popularity, a
patriotic impulse to paint a portrait of Washington brought him

1. "Masters in Art: Stuart," January, 1906.

--◦∙❮ 47 ❯∙◦--

back to this country. He worked in New York, Philadelphia, Washington, and finally settled in Boston.

His portraiture was enhanced by his capacity to create an environment which banished self-consciousness in his sitters, a feat he achieved largely through his personal charm. His portraits, the best of which are superb—the flesh, brilliant and transparent in the light, mellow yet glowing in the shadows—have a permanent freshness and are painted with unequalled purity of color. At times there are suggestions of fabric or lace, but these were indicated merely to give an effect, and in general costumes were but accessories. He said himself "I copy the works of God, and leave the clothes to tailors and mantua-makers."

In 1825 Stuart's health began to fail, and he died on July 9, 1828. The "Life and Works of Gilbert Stuart," by George C. Mason, attributing more than six hundred portraits to this indefatigable artist, remained for some time the best work of reference on Stuart's life. It is now superseded by Lawrence Park's monumental work on Stuart.

Among the Jewish portraits is the typical Stuart head of Abraham Touro, brother of the philanthropist Judah Touro, of New Orleans and Boston, and son of Isaac Touro, whose portrait Stuart painted from memory after Touro's death. The Touro family were early residents of Newport, and Ezra Stiles, in his diary, mentions spending the day, June 30, 1773, with Mr. Abraham de Isaac Touro, who married a Miss Hays,[1] and for whom Rabbi Karigal performed the ceremony.

Dr. I. M. Cline, of New Orleans, the present owner of this portrait,[2] said that it was given by Judah Touro to Mr. Gershom

1. Miss Reyna Hays was a sister of Moses Michael Hays.
2. This portrait was just acquired, March, 1927, by The Ehrich Galleries, New York.

Kursheedt, of New Orleans, who had been appointed executor of the Touro estate. Mr. Kursheedt gave it to his sister, Mrs. Benjamin Florance (née Rebecca Kursheedt, of New Orleans), who passed it to her son, Mr. Ernest Touro Florance, from whom it was purchased by Dr. Cline. The portrait is that of a very handsome young man, keen of visage, pleasing in expression. Doctor Cline writes that he has seen many Stuarts, but this cannot be surpassed for subtlety and charm.

Mr. Touro, at the age of forty-five, while watching a parade in Boston one day, met with a fatal accident, having crushed his leg in leaping from his chaise. In his will this young man, among other legacies, left ten thousand dollars to the Massachusetts General Hospital and fifteen thousand dollars to the synagogue at Newport, where his body is interred.

Another Stuart portrait is that of Jacob Rodriguez Rivera, painted about 1774 and given by Miss Rodman, of Boston, to the Redwood Library in Newport. The Rodman family records reveal that the painting is that of Jacob Rivera and not of Abraham, as has been commonly supposed. Miss Rodman's great-grandfather Rodman lived as a youth in Newport, where the Jews employed advanced business methods then unknown to other members of the community, and young men who sought superior commercial training attached themselves to the Jewish merchants there. Mr. Rodman entered the employ of Jacob Rivera and, admiring his character and personality, asked him to sit for his portrait.[1] There has been some dispute as to the authenticity of this portrait.[2] Miss Rodman believes that it was painted by Edward

1. Conversation with Miss Emma Rodman, Boston.

2. "Mr. Hart examined this Rivera portrait with me and decided that it was painted by Savage and not by Stuart. I did not agree with him, nor did Miss Rodman, at that time at least. What Mr. Bayley's opinion about it is I do not know."—Lawrence Park.

Savage in Leicester, Massachusetts, where her family afterward lived, and where, too, she believes the Riveras removed, but Mr. Frank W. Bayley, after a study of the historic data available and examination of the technique, said that it was painted by Stuart in his early period. The portrait is that of a gentleman past middle life in a black coat, wearing a white stock collar and white lace cuffs. His right hand rests on the back of a draped chair, and his left hand is tucked inside his coat. The face is very well drawn, showing a prominent nose and protruding lower lip. The artist, with feeling and sincerity, has reproduced the character and personality of the gentle gray-haired old man. It is a striking example of early American art.

Another important Stuart is that of Samuel Myers, the son of Myer Myers, a banker and the foremost New York silversmith of his day. Samuel was born in New York City, in 1775. Because of the political activities of the elder Myers in behalf of the Revolutionists, the family was forced to flee to Connecticut upon the occupation of New York by the British. The Samuel Myers portrait was painted for him by Gilbert Stuart about 1810, when Myers was living in Richmond, Virginia, where he went after his marriage in 1796 to his second wife, Judith Hays, of Boston.[1] The portrait is now owned by a great-granddaughter, Mrs. John Hill Morgan of New York City. It is on a mahogany panel twenty-five by thirty inches, and a copy, possibly by Jane Stuart, a daughter of the artist, is owned by Mrs. Morgan's sister, Mrs. Richard Frothingham O'Neil, of Boston. Against a red background is limned the portrait of a distinguished-looking man of middle age, his hair tinged with gray, wearing a black coat, white stock collar, and a lace-

1. Letters from John Hill Morgan, Esq., New York.

ruffled shirt. His nose is aquiline, his mouth firm and small, and he has a large chin and forehead. The eyes, appraising yet kindly, are indicative of a character that reached great heights both in commerce and in philanthropy.

At the time Mr. Myers gave the commission for his own picture, he ordered from Stuart a replica of his Athenæum portrait of Washington, for whom Mr. Myers had conceived a great admiration. He owned this picture for many years, when he either sold or presented it to the Virginia State Library. This Washington portrait, however, has unfortunately disappeared.

Judah Hays, 1772–1832, a brother-in-law of Samuel Myers, was also painted by Stuart at the same time, probably at the request of Mr. Myers. The portrait descended to a grandson, Major E. T. D. Myers, of Richmond, Virginia (for many years President of the Richmond, Fredericksburg & Potomac Railway Company), at whose home, in a fire, it was badly damaged some ten years ago. It has been restored and is now in the possession of another descendant, Mrs. William C. Preston, of Richmond, Virginia. Mrs. O'Neil has a copy of this portrait painted by her father, Mr. William Myers, an artist, which Mr. Morgan believes is superior to the burned original.

Judah, the son of Moses Michael Hays, of Boston, received a good education, which was further enhanced by the study of French in Europe, whither he set out in 1796. Subsequent trips were made there on business, and on the death of his father he inherited a fortune representing large real estate holdings. To him belongs the distinction of being one of the founders of the Boston Athenæum. Possessed of wealth and culture, it is unfortunate that he did not live longer to enjoy its benefits; his life was cut short, while on a pleasure trip to Florida, by an accidental drowning. His portrait represents a handsome young man of romantic countenance, with wavy brown hair and blue eyes and regular features.

The Myers family are represented in other portraits by Stuart now owned by Mr. Barton Myers, of Norfolk, Virginia. These are the portraits of Mr. and Mrs. Moses Myers, which have been incorrectly listed in Mason's book under the name "Mieres."

Mr. Myers' portrait was painted about 1808 in Boston. He is seated in a gilded armchair, upholstered in crimson velvet, before a table covered with a crimson cloth, on which his right hand rests holding an open letter. His hair is powdered, his eyes are dark brown, and he wears short side whiskers. His white neckcloth, tie, shirt frills, and white waistcoat are in accordance with the gentlemanly attire of the day. His eyebrows and forehead suggest a largesse of thought, and the appearance of whimsicality and discernment — in the eyes and mouth — affirms a definitely Jewish expression.

Moses Myers was the son of Hyman Myers, a native of Amsterdam, who resided in New York. Moses came to Norfolk, Virginia, in 1786. He was a foremost citizen of Norfolk, and a Jewish banker there. When the Bank of Richmond was established in 1792, he was named in the act as its superintendent at Norfolk. He also represented the French Republic at Norfolk at this critical time. An old record says of Moses Myers: "He possessed in an eminent degree what may be called the chivalry of the commercial character, and displayed in bearing a dignity and grace which looked infinitely beyond an ignoble rivalry and the tricks of trade."

His wife was Eliza Judd or Judah of Montreal, the daughter of Samuel Judah, who, though living in Canada during the Revolution, sympathized with the American cause, and rendered it invaluable service.

Eliza's portrait was also painted about 1808 in Boston. Clustered beneath a white turban are seen little reddish-brown curls, and a lace shawl delicately falls over her low-necked Empire dress. Stuart made little of accessories and backgrounds, and here, as in the portraits of so many women whom he painted, Mrs. Myers is seated in an Empire armchair—a studio property—with a gilded wooden frame and upholstered in crimson velvet.

There hangs in the Pennsylvania Academy of Fine Arts, the portrait of Colonel Isaac Franks, presented to him with this inscription: "Portrait of Mr. Isaac Franks presented to friend Isaac Franks as a token of regard by Gilbert Stuart, Germantown, October 1, 1802." The portrait was left to Samuel and Sara Franks, children of the Colonel, each by turn to have it for one year. The picture was afterwards sold by G. W. Huffnagel, son-in-law of Colonel Franks, to the late Henry C. Gibson, who bequeathed it to the Museum.

Isaac Franks was a great patriot and officer in the Revolutionary Army. He was born in New York, May 27, 1759, and died in Philadelphia, March 4, 1822. It was in his house at Germantown, a suburb of Philadelphia, that President Washington resided during the prevalence of the yellow fever.

A Stuart portrait of surpassing beauty in the possession of Mr. Henry Joseph of Montreal, Canada, is of the beautiful Rachel Gratz, daughter of Michael Gratz, and sister of Rebecca Gratz. It is almost impossible to set down in words the unusual charm of her face with its expressive eyes and delicate features, the graceful sweep of her blond curls, the contour of her neck and shoulders, all of which combine to make a portrait of surpassing loveliness. In comparison with her sister, Rebecca, she had no "history." She married Solomon Moses in 1806, also portrayed by Stuart, reared a large family, and died at the age of forty in 1823.

The portrait of her husband was painted in 1806. Solomon Moses was no less handsome than his beautiful wife, Rachel Gratz; indeed, there are few Stuart portraits with which these do not favorably compare. In the refined oval of the face, the glowing eyes, the chiselled nose, mouth, and chin, the absolute freedom and life quality of the pose, is the quintessence of Stuart's art. Solomon Moses was a merchant of no small importance in New York, by 1796, and he and his wife reared a large family, of which a daughter, Sarah Gratz Moses, was the mother of Mr. Joseph, the present owner of the portrait.

Another Stuart in this collection is that of Mrs. Michael Gratz, the mother-in-law of Solomon Moses. Mrs. Gratz was Miriam Simon, the daughter of Joseph Simon. She was born in 1750 and died in 1808. Mrs. Gratz is shown with a dainty lace cap, worn by the mothers of that generation, a thin white fichu about her throat, and hands folded in matronly fashion. Common sense gleams from those clear eyes and intelligent countenance, a thoroughly practical and livable character of dignity and calm, modelled with care and elegance.

The Gratz family is also represented by another artist in this collection in the portrait of Joseph Gratz, 1785–1858, the son of Mr. and Mrs. Michael Gratz, by George Peter Alexander Healy. Healy was born in Boston, in 1808, and at his best his portraits, especially those of eminent men, among whom are Webster, Clay, and Calhoun, are full of vigor, and rank with notable examples of

American portraiture. This portrait of Gratz is unmistakably a rugged piece of work, a characterization of a dignified looking man in a dark suit and white collar. He was secretary of the Congregation Mikve Israel for a long period of time in Philadelphia, was a director of the Institution for the Instruction of the Deaf and Dumb in that city, and an early member of the first City Troop of the Philadelphia Club. Like his brothers Hyman and Simon, he remained unmarried. In view of the numerous and interesting details of the Gratz family, it is surprising that more of his life has not been recorded. His sister Rebecca and his father Michael Gratz are immortalized in portraits by Sully in the collection of Mr. Henry Joseph of Montreal.

Thomas Sully, 1783–1872, was born in England and came to this country with his family when nine years of age. When twenty years old, having failed in business, he established himself as an artist, and after a short residence in New York and in Boston where he received some instruction from Gilbert Stuart, returned to London, where he studied with Benjamin West. On his return he did some excellent portraits, and in 1837 made another visit to England, during which he painted the celebrated portrait of Queen Victoria. His best work, however, was done before 1825, most of his pictures after that degenerating into mere prettiness. However, his work at its best reveals a singular charm and delicacy. In his long life of eighty-nine years he painted hundreds of portraits listed in his Register.[1] Among them are a number of Jewish portraits, but only a few can be described here.

1. See addenda. Doubtless there were many Jews painted by Sully whom I have not listed, because wherever there has been a shadow of doubt I have deemed it best to omit them. It is not alone from the name that one can discover a Jewish origin. In Pennsylvania, for example, there were families of German and Dutch origin whose names might have applied equally to Jew or Gentile.

The brilliant youth of Rebecca Gratz, so charmingly portrayed in the Malbone miniatures, was fulfilled in a life devoted to charity and philanthropy, and in Mr. Joseph's large painting of her by Sully[1] much of this loveliness of character finds expression. She has an olive complexion, brilliant color, soft, dark brown eyes and black hair. Over her claret-colored dress she wears a white lace drape and a pale yellow mantle lined with white fur.[2] That this was a faithful representation of the subject is confirmed by John Sartain in his "Reminiscences of a very Old man," in which he tells of a visit to Miss Gratz in her later life. "Her eyes struck me as piercingly dark, yet of mild expression, in a face tenderly pale. The portrait Sully painted of her must have been a remarkable likeness, that so many years after I should recognize her instantly by remembrance of it."

Her father, Michael Gratz, 1740–1811, came to America in 1758 and settled in Philadelphia. A description of the portrait by the present owner singles out especially the blue eyes, ruddy complexion and gray hair, the buff waistcoat, white stock and taupe coat.[3] The so-called looseness which mars some of Sully's other portraits finds no place here. In this magnificent portrayal of a keen and kindly-visaged man, Sully has achieved a remarkable study. It betrays no sentimentality; it is the face of a man of strong character, not insensitive to beauty and permeated with nobility. Some of the extraordinary business enterprise and initiative which among other things impelled him to purchase the Mammoth Cave in Kentucky has found expression in this painting.

The colonizing impulse came upon him in the years between

1. See addenda for other Sully portraits of Rebecca Gratz.
2. Letters from Henry Joseph, Esq., Montreal.
3. Letters from Henry Joseph, Esq., Montreal.

1768–1775, and he engaged in many enterprises which were continued by his son Benjamin Gratz, 1792–1884; and their collected documents from the time of the Seven Years' War to the Revolution, from the War of 1812 to the Mexican and Civil Wars, compass the growth of the United States not only from the Atlantic Coast to the Mississippi, but even to the Rio Grande and the Pacific. Benjamin finally took up his residence at Lexington, Kentucky, and became second president of the first Kentucky railroad. He married Maria Cecil Gist, granddaughter of Christopher Gist, whose maps, now in the Public Record Office in London, are the first on record from actual surveys of the Ohio Valley. His portrait and that of his wife were both painted by Sully, and are in the possession of a daughter, Mrs. Thomas Clay of Lexington, Kentucky, whose husband was a grandson of Henry Clay.

Sully's Register includes the portrait of Gustavus A. Myers, 1801–1869, the son of Samuel Myers, of whom the portrait by Stuart has already been mentioned. Gustavus married Mrs. James Hugh Conway, the daughter of Governor William Giles of Virginia. He and his father lived in adjoining houses in Richmond, and the well-known Crump House there is the house once owned by Samuel Myers. A son, William, was a talented artist, who copied the Stuart portrait of his great-uncle Judah Hays, and the Sully portrait of his father. Gustavus was a prominent lawyer and a man of pronounced literary tastes, and thus drew about him a circle of friends, one of whom was G. P. R. James, for several years British Consul in Richmond. At the outbreak of the Civil War, no doubt through the recommendation of Mr. James, Mr. Myers was appointed British Consul in Richmond and, though not an official minister, acted as representative of the British Government in its dealings with the Confederate States of America throughout the war.[1]

In the portrait by Sully the face is illumined with a fine spiritual quality. It is owned by Mr. Myers' granddaughter, Mrs. John Hill Morgan of Brooklyn, and for some time has been on exhibition at the Brooklyn Art Museum together with the Stuart portrait of Samuel Myers.

Sully was known as the "Sir Thomas Lawrence of America" because, in his charming and delicate portrayal of women, he was not unlike his great English contemporary. The delicacy of his brush is exemplified in a portrait, owned by the Corcoran Gallery of Art, of Fanny Yates, who was born in Liverpool, England, of a prominent Jewish family. Here she was married to Jacob Clavius Levy, a native of Charleston, South Carolina, when she was but sixteen years of age, and came to this country with her husband about 1840. Jacob Clavius was a gentleman of note; he was a director of the Union Insurance Company from 1830–1840, a delegate to the Knoxville R. R. Convention in 1836, and a member of the Charleston Chamber of Commerce from 1841–1847. Politically he was affiliated with the Union party. A scholarly article which he wrote on the "Reformed Israelites" appeared in *The Southern Quarterly Review* for April, 1844. His father, an Englishman by birth, came to this country at an early age, bringing with him books, silverware, glass and china.[2]

Mr. and Mrs. Jacob Clavius Levy reared a large family. A daughter, Eugenia, married Philip Phillips, a lawyer of prominence, who originated the Court of Claims. Eugenia, a brilliant

1. Letters from John Hill Morgan, Esq., New York.
2. Letters from Mrs. Eugenia Phillips Myers Minis, the great-granddaughter of Fanny Yates Levy.

woman, was a member of a select and noted coterie of Washington society from 1850–1860. During the war between the States, she was arrested twice on account of her strong southern sympathies. A son, Samuel Yates Levy, was a lawyer in Savannah, Georgia, and the author of several plays, one of which, the "Italian Bride," was performed.

Fanny Yates Levy died at the home of her daughter, Mrs. George Repplier, in Philadelphia, when she was ninety-four years old. She was buried in Savannah, Georgia, where her family removed in 1848.

Thomas Sully painted Mrs. Levy's portrait in 1842, a few years after her arrival in Charleston. Her small and well-shaped head, with its luminous dark brown eyes, is turned slightly to the right, and over her brown hair, parted in the middle, is a gray headdress which softly falls to her shoulders. The portrait is a symphony in brown and gray tones relieved by the rosy hues of her olive complexion.

The portrait of Major Alfred Mordecai also belongs to the long list of American Jews who were patrons of Sully. Alfred Mordecai, the son of Jacob Mordecai, whose portrait was painted by Jarvis, was born in North Carolina in 1804. When fifteen years of age he was admitted to West Point, from which he was graduated, at the head of his class, in 1823. He then became an instructor and author on military subjects and published "Experiments on Gunpowder" and other works. As a recognized authority in the military world, his fame spread throughout the country and abroad. He was sent by our government to the Crimea in 1855–1857 to witness operations there, and his report was published by order of Congress. From 1823–1861 he was an executive officer of the

Staff Corps of the Army, in which he had attained the rank of Major, but at the outbreak of the Civil War he resigned, as he was a southerner by birth and sentiment, and refrained from taking any active part in the war. Major Mordecai married Anne Hays, a devout Jewess, who was the granddaughter of Michael Gratz and the great-granddaughter of Joseph Simon of Lancaster. He died in Philadelphia in 1887. His portrait, expressing in the deep-set eyes and firmly moulded chin a person of strength and determination, is in the possession of his daughter, Miss Mordecai, of Philadelphia.

Another Sully portrait is that of Solomon Jacobs, who was born in 1775. He lived in Richmond, Virginia, a very wealthy, prominent, and respected citizen. Besides his own home, which was on the south side of Grace Street between Eighth and Ninth Streets, he owned some of the most desirable property in Richmond. He also represented the French government in the tobacco market and acted as local agent for the banking house of Rothschild. At one time he was Recorder and Acting Mayor, the highest municipal office ever held by a Richmond Jew. On December 11, 1810, he was elected Grand Master of the Masons of Virginia and retired December 14, 1813, after three consecutive years, which has been, as far as known, the longest period ever served by any Grand Master. His lodge was the Richmond Randolph, number nineteen. Solomon Jacobs' portrait was recently sold by the Macbeth Gallery to Mrs. William Averell Harriman of New York.

Sully painted a second portrait of Solomon Jacobs in his Masonic regalia. This has been engraved by I. A. O'Neill. Mr. F. Boykin Jacobs, of Richmond, Virginia, his grandson, wrote me the following about the portrait: "I am not sure whether it was painted in Philadelphia or Richmond as my grandfather lived in Philadelphia before settling here. The background is dark brown, and the colors are most beautifully brought out. The painting was sent on to New York City some years ago, where it was awarded a prize as one of Sully's masterpieces. It was sent by the Masons, as he was Grand Master of Masons of the State of Virginia. This is all the information I can give as our family records were destroyed at the evacuation of Richmond in April, 1865."

The Levy family, prominent in the social and communal life of Philadelphia, were also patrons of Sully. Samson Levy, Senior, 1722–1781, was a merchant and one of the founders of the City Dancing Assembly of Philadelphia, and his eight children by inheritance became members of this exclusive assembly. The eldest, Moses, 1758–1826, was a famous lawyer and judge, whose portrait, painted by Rembrandt Peale, has already been mentioned.

Moses' daughters, Henrietta and Martha, painted by Sully in 1810, are still in their original frames. Henrietta's portrait is in the possession of Mr. J. J. Milligan, and Martha's is owned by her granddaughter, Mrs. Robert Hale Bancroft, of Boston.[1] It is a charming portrait of a young girl of twelve, in a high-waisted dress with a rose girdle, standing by a brown spinet, quaint and demure and with rather uncommon poise, if we may call it such, for a girl of her tender years.

Portraits by Sully of Samson Levy, Junior, 1761–1831, and of his wife, who was Sarah Coates, are also in the Bancroft home. Samson was an interesting, yet eccentric character. As a lawyer he was conspicuous more for his brilliancy and eloquence than for his knowledge of the law. He was evidently a lover of the arts, as

1. Conversation with Mrs. Robert Hale Bancroft, Boston.

his portrait was painted not only by Sully, but also drawn by St. Mémin, and he was one of the incorporators of the Pennsylvania Academy of Fine Arts. It is interesting to note here that Samson and Moses Levy were the grandsons of Moses Levy, of New York, whose daughter Bilhah Abigail married Jacob Franks. Their portraits in the collection of the Hon. N. Taylor Phillips have already been spoken of. The revelation of these portraits was in the nature of a surprise to Mrs. Bancroft, as she was quite unaware of their existence.

The fabric of romance is thus woven by these old portraits from ancestor to descendant. The story of that romance, if it could be told in its entirety, would constitute a fascinating chapter in the annals of our country. There must still be countless portraits among the descendants of the early American Jews hanging, unknown, upon the walls of old mansions or galleries, or hidden in garrets and sequestered corners, for nearly every man of means had a portrait painted of himself or of his relatives in an age when the characters and records of families were conveyed as much through the brush as through the pen. It is well that the memoirs of these people should be preserved, for among them were Jews who made notable contributions to the history of our country, and in the absence of photographs and documentary records, these old portraits have a special significance, not merely from the sentimental point of view, but from their artistic and historical aspects.

IV

ADDENDA

SINCE there is no available record of the portraits of early American Jews, I have thought it advisable to put into form whatever data I have been able to gather as a basis for further additions and discoveries which may appear from time to time. Except where otherwise indicated, the following, so far as I know, are portraits in oil.

Record of Portraits

BAER

Israel B. Kursheedt, 1776–1852. Painted about 1846.
Owned by the Misses Kursheedt, New York.

This portrait is reproduced in a Masonic publication, "Robert W. Reid, Washington Lodge No. 21, A. F. and A. M., New York, 1911."

WILLIAM HENRY BROWN

John Moss, 1771–1847. Silhouette. Attributed to Brown.
Owned by J. Bunford Samuel, Esq., Philadelphia.

ROBERT FEKE

Mrs. Barnard Gratz (Richea Mears or Meyers), 1731–1801. Attributed to Feke by Lawrence Park.
Owned by Dr. I. Minis Hays, Philadelphia.

CHARLES BALTHAZAR JULIEN FEVRET
DE ST. MÉMIN

Henry Alexander. Lived in Baltimore. Drawing made in 1803.

Abraham Hart. Lived in New York. Drawing made in 1796.

Samson Levy, Jr., 1761–1831. Son of Samson and Martha (Lampley) Levy. Drawing made in 1802.

 Owned by Mrs. Robert Hale Bancroft, Boston.

Mrs. Samson Levy (Sarah Coates). Wife of Samson Levy, Jr. Drawing made in 1802.

 Mrs. Albert Bache, Philadelphia, has in her possession a small engraving of Mrs. Levy reduced from the original portrait.

Mrs. Samson Levy (Martha Lampley), 1731–1807. Mother of Samson Levy, Jr. Drawing made in 1802.

 Owned by Mrs. Robert Hale Bancroft, Boston.

Hyman Marks. Lived in Richmond, Va. Drawing made in 1805.

 Collection of the American Jewish Historical Society.

Solomon Moses. Lived in New York. Drawing made in 1796.

CHARLES FRASER

Octavius Cohen. Painted 1836. Miniature.

 This miniature is listed in "Early American Portrait Painters in Miniature," by Theodore Bolton.

Mrs. Mordecai (Lucretia Cohen). Painted 1834. Miniature.

 Same as above.

CHESTER P. HARDING

Hayman Levy, (?)–1865. Painted 1838.

 Owned by Bunford Samuel, Esq., Philadelphia.

Mrs. Hayman Levy (Almeria De Leon), 1799–1879, and Child. Painted 1839.

 Owned by Bunford Samuel, Esq., Philadelphia.

GEORGE PETER ALEXANDER HEALY

Hyman Gratz, 1776–1857.

 Owned by Henry Joseph, Esq., Montreal, Canada.

Joseph Gratz, 1758–1858.

 Owned by Henry Joseph, Esq., Montreal, Canada.

ADDENDA

JAMES HERRING

Naphtali Phillips, 1772–1870.
  Owned by Hon. N. Taylor Phillips, New York.

DANIEL HUNTINGTON

Seixas Nathan, 1785–1852.
  Owned by Clarence S. Nathan, Esq., New York.

EMMA INMAN

M. B. Seixas. Painted about 1840.
  Owned by John F. Braun, Esq., Philadelphia, Pa.

HENRY INMAN

Simon Nathan, 1746–1822. Water Color. Patriot in Revolution.
  Owned by Mrs. Annie Nathan Meyer, New York.

Simon Nathan, 1746–1822.
  Owned by Miss Sarah Lyons, New York.

Mrs. Simon Nathan (Grace Seixas), 1752–1831. Water Color.
  Owned by Mrs. Annie Nathan Meyer, New York.

JOHN WESLEY JARVIS

Solomon Etting, 1764–1847. 26½ x 33 inches.
  Collection of Maryland Historical Society.

Mrs. Solomon Etting (Rachel Gratz), 1764–1831. 26½ x 32 inches.
  Collection of Maryland Historical Society.

Jacob Mordecai, 1762–1838.
  Owned by Professor Samuel Mordecai, Durham, N. C.

Major Mordecai Myers, 1776–1870.
  The owner of the original portrait is not known to me. The portrait is reproduced in "Biographical Sketches of the Bailey-Myers-Mason Families, 1776–1905."

Mordecai M. Noah, 1785–1851. 30 x 48 inches.
  Owned by Robert L. Noah, Esq., New York.

R. JEAN

? Jacobs. Drawing made in 1813.
   Owned by Bunford Samuel, Esq., Philadelphia.

JACOB H. LAZARUS

Aaron Lopez Gomez, ?–1860.
   Owned by Mrs. Walter A. Dreyfous, New York.
Mrs. Aaron Lopez Gomez (Hetty Hendricks), ?–1865.
   Owned by Mrs. Walter A. Dreyfous, New York.
Mrs. Mordecai M. Noah, ?–?.
   Owned by Robert L. Noah, Esq., New York.

EDWARD GREENE MALBONE

Rachel Gratz, 1783–1823. Miniature.
   Owned by Mrs. John Hunter, Savannah, Ga.
Rebecca Gratz, 1781–1869. Miniature.
   Owned by Miss Rachel Gratz Nathan, New York.
David Moses. Miniature.
   Owned by Miss Rachel Gratz Nathan, New York.
Mrs. Jacob Myers (Miriam Etting), 1787–1808. Miniature. 2 x 4 inches.
   Collection of the Maryland Historical Society.

CHARLES WILLSON PEALE

Colonel David Salisbury Franks, ?–about 1794. Painted 1776. Miniature.
   Owned by Mrs. Clarence I. De Sola, Montreal, Canada.
Jonas Phillips, 1736–1803. Attributed to Peale.
   Collection of the American Jewish Historical Society, New York.
Mrs. Jonas Phillips (Rebecca Machado), 1746–1831. Attributed to Peale.
   Owned by Isaac Graff, Esq., New York.
   There is a copy of this portrait in the collection of the American Jewish Historical Society.

JAMES PEALE

Frances Etting, 1771–?.
   Dinmore of Philadelphia, October, 1858, photographed the original portrait, which I have not been able to trace.
Reuben Etting, 1762–1848.
   Same as above.

REMBRANDT PEALE

Judge Moses Levy, 1758–1826.
    Owned by J. J. Milligan, Esq., Baltimore, Md.
Mrs. Moses Levy (Mary Pearce), 1763–1850.
    Owned by J. J. Milligan, Esq., Baltimore, Md.
Mrs. Mordecai Sheftall (Frances Hart). Living in Charleston, S. C.,
    1779. Miniature.
    Owned by Mrs. W. M. Brickner, New York.

EDWARD F. PETTICOLAS

Elihu Etting. Painted 1799. Miniature.
    Owned by the Pennsylvania Academy of Fine Arts.

CHARLES PEALE POLK

Barnard Gratz, 1738–1801.
    Owned by Dr. I. Minis Hays, Philadelphia, Pa.

JOHN RAMAGE

Joseph Simson, 1686–1787. Miniature.
    Owned by Mrs. Ansel Leo, Yonkers, New York.
    This portrait has been reproduced in "Publications of the American Jewish
    Historical Society," Vol. 27.

THOMAS BUCHANAN READ

Commodore Uriah P. Levy, 1792–1862. Attributed to Read.
Collection of Thomas Jefferson Home, at Monticello, Va.

SIR JOSHUA REYNOLDS[1]

Miss Franks, ?–1802. Portrait of a child fondling a lamb. Daughter of
    Aaron Franks. Married Moses Franks.

Moses Franks. Living in London in 1781. He was probably the brother
    of the well-known Rebecca Franks, as her brother, Moses, was
    living in London at this time.
    Photographic copies from the portraits of Miss Franks and Moses Franks are in
    the possession of the American Jewish Historical Society.

---

1. Although painted by an English artist, the subjects are listed on account of the particular interest
attached to this family.

JAMES SHARPLES

Samuel Hays, 1764–1839. Pastel.
Owned by Dr. I Minis Hays, Philadelphia, Pa.

SEIXAS

Mrs. Michael Marks (Johaveth Isaacs), 1767–1852.
Owned by Amelia J. Allen, Philadelphia, Pa.

J. H. SHEGOGUE

Jacob Hays, 1772–1830. 40 x 50 inches. High Constable of New York.
Collection of the New York City Hall, Aldermanic Rooms.

JOHN SMIBERT

Rabbi Raphael Haijm Karigal, 1733–1777.
A likeness of Karigal on ivory, probably by Smibert, was given to the late Rev. Jacques Judah Lyons. See "Publications of the American Jewish Historical Society," Vol. 27, BII, pages 63–64.

F. R. SPENCER

Mrs. Joseph Andrews (Sally Salomon), 1779–1854. Daughter of Haym
  Salomon. Painted 1846.
Owned by Miss Gertrude Dreyfous, New York.

GILBERT STUART

Colonel Isaac Franks, 1759–1822. Painted in Germantown, 1802. Canvas,
  29 x 24 inches.
Owned by the Pennsylvania Academy of Fine Arts.
Mrs. Michael Gratz (Miriam Simon), 1750–1808. Painted in Phila-
  delphia, 1802. Canvas, 28 x 24 inches. Half-length, seated.
Owned by Henry Joseph, Esq,. Montreal, Canada.
Judah Hays, 1772–1832. Painted in Boston about 1810. Panel, 27¾ x 23
  inches.
Owned by Mrs. William C. Preston, Richmond, Va.
This portrait was partially destroyed, but has been restored. Mrs. Richard Frothingham O'Neil of Boston owns a copy of the original portrait.

Isaac Moses, 1742–1818. Father of Solomon Moses. Canvas, 30 x 25 inches. Seated.

> Owned by Miss Rachel Gratz Nathan, New York.

This portrait has been reproduced in "Publications of the American Jewish Historical Society," Vol. 27.

Solomon Moses, 1774–1857. Painted 1796. Canvas, 28 x 24 inches. Seated.

> Owned by Henry Joseph, Esq., Montreal, Canada.

Mrs. Solomon Moses (Rachel Gratz), 1783–1823. Painted in 1806. Canvas, 28 x 24 inches. Seated.

> Owned by Henry Joseph, Esq., Montreal, Canada.

Moses Myers. Painted about 1808. Panel, 33 x 26¼ inches. Half-length, seated.

> Owned by Barton Myers, Esq., Norfolk, Va.

This portrait is listed as "Mr. Mieres" in Mason's book, "Life and Works of Gilbert Stuart," on page 223.

Mrs. Moses Myers (Eliza Judd or Judah). Painted about 1808. Panel, 33 x 26¼ inches. Half-length, seated.

> Owned by Barton Myers, Esq., Norfolk, Va.

This portrait is also listed in Mason on page 223 as "Mrs. Mieres."

Samuel Myers, 1775–1836. Painted about 1810. Panel, 25 x 30 inches. Bust.

> Owned by Mrs. John Hill Morgan, Brooklyn, New York.

A copy is in the possession of Mrs. Richard Frothingham O'Neil, Boston. The original portrait is now on exhibition at the Brooklyn Art Museum.

Jacob Rodriguez Rivera, 1717–1789. Painted about 1774. Canvas, 34½ x 27¼ inches. Half-length, seated.

> Collection of Redwood Library, Newport, R. I.

Abraham Touro, 1777–1822. Canvas, 27 x 22 inches. Bust.

> Owned by The Ehrich Galleries, New York.

There is another Stuart portrait of Touro in the Massachusetts General Hospital, Boston, and the replica of this portrait is owned by Samuel W. Weis, Esq., Chicago.

Isaac Touro. Father of Abraham and Judah Touro.

There is no trace of this portrait which Stuart painted from memory after Touro's death.

THOMAS SULLY

Miss Etting. Painted 1808.
> This portrait is listed in "Life and Works of Thomas Sully," by Biddle and Fielding.

Miss Sally Etting. Painted 1808. 25 x 30 inches.
> Owned by Mr. Frank M. Etting, Philadelphia, Pa.

Mrs. Solomon Etting (Rachel Gratz), 1764–1831. Painted 1835.
> This portrait is listed in "Life and Works of Thomas Sully," by Biddle and Fielding.

Benjamin Gratz, 1792–1884. Painted 1831. 17 x 20 inches.
> Owned by Mrs. Thomas Clay, Lexington, Ky.

Mrs. Benjamin Gratz (Maria Cecil Gist), ?–1841.
> Owned by Mrs. Thomas Clay, Lexington, Ky.

Michael Gratz, 1740–1811. Painted 1808.
> Owned by Henry Joseph, Esq., Montreal, Canada.

Rebecca Gratz, 1781–1869. Painted 1831. 25 x 30 inches.
> Owned by Henry Joseph, Esq., Montreal, Canada.

Rebecca Gratz, 1781–1869. Painted 1807.
> This portrait was copied from a miniature by Edward Greene Malbone, for Thomas A. Cooper, 1807. See "Life and Works of Thomas Sully," Biddle and Fielding.

Rebecca Gratz, 1781–1869. Painting begun 1830. 16 x 19 inches.
> Owned by John Gribbel, Esq., Philadelphia, Pa.
> This portrait painted for Hyman Gratz was noted in Sully's Register as "erased." However, it was probably finished. The portrait shows Miss Gratz wearing a turban or head-dress painted in by the artist. There is a tradition in the Gratz family that it was not accepted on that account.

Rebecca Gratz, 1781–1869. Painted 1831. 17 x 20 inches.
> Owned by Mrs. Thomas Clay, Lexington, Ky.
> A copy of this portrait by a Kentucky artist hangs in the Jewish Foster Home, Germantown, Pa.

Mrs. Isaac Hays (Sarah Anna Minis), 1811–1884. Painted 1833. 17 x 20 inches.
> Owned by Mrs. Sarah Minis Goodrich, Princeton, N. J.

Solomon Jacobs, 1775–1827.
> Owned by Mrs. William Averell Harriman, New York.

Solomon Jacobs, 1775–1827. Painted 1812, in Masonic regalia.
> Owned by F. Boykin Jacobs, Esq., Richmond, Va.
> This portrait was engraved by I. A. O'Neill.

Mrs. S. Jacobs. Painted 1815.
> The owner of this portrait is not known to me. It is listed in Sully's Register.

Miss Henrietta Levy, 1792–1860. Daughter of Judge Moses Levy. Painted 1810. 20 x 24 inches.
> Owned by J. J. Milligan, Esq., Baltimore, Md.

Mrs. Jacob Clavius Levy (Fanny Yates). Painted in 1842.
> Owned by the Corcoran Gallery of Art.

Miss Martha Levy, 1798–?. Daughter of Judge Moses Levy. Painted 1810. 19 x 23 inches.
> Owned by Mrs. Robert Hale Bancroft, Boston.
> This portrait was loaned to the Boston Museum of Fine Arts (1920).

Samson Levy, Jr., 1761–1831. Brother of Judge Moses Levy. Painted 1808. 24¼ x 29½ inches.
> Owned by Mrs. Robert Hale Bancroft, Boston.
> This portrait was loaned to the Boston Museum of Fine Arts (1920).

Mrs. Samson Levy, Jr. (Sarah Coates). Painted 1808. 24¼ x 29½ inches.
> Owned by Mrs. Robert Hale Bancroft, Boston.
> This portrait was loaned to the Boston Museum of Fine Arts (1920).

Mrs. Hyman Marks, ?–?. Miniature.
> Owned by Grace N. Lederer, Philadelphia.

Major Alfred Mordecai, 1804–1887. Painted 1836. 17 x 20 inches.
> Owned by Miss Mordecai, Philadelphia.

Mr. Moses "of New York," 1753–1843. Painted 1808.
> Owned by Miss Rachel Gratz Nathan, New York.
> This portrait of Mr. Moses listed in Sully's Register is probably that of Moses I. or L. Moses, brother of Isaac Moses. According to Miss Gratz it was painted by Sully, but Lawrence Park has attributed the portrait to Gilbert Stuart.

Mrs. Solomon Moses (Rachel Gratz), 1783–1823.
> Owned by Miss Rachel Gratz Nathan, New York.

Gustavus A. Myers, 1801–1869. Painted 1865. 21 x 25 inches.
> Owned by Mrs. John Hill Morgan, Brooklyn, New York.
> This portrait is now on exhibition at the Brooklyn Art Museum.

Mr. Myers. Lived in Norfolk, Va. Painted 1808.
> This portrait is that of John Myers, owned by Barton Myers, Esq., of Norfolk, Va.

Miss Nones. Painted 1815.
> The owner of this portrait is not known to me. It is listed in Sully's Register.

JEREMIAH THEUS

Manuel Josephson, 1729–1796.
  Owned by Dr. I. Minis Hays, Philadelphia.
Mrs. Manuel Josephson (Ritzel Judah), ?–?.
  Owned by Dr. I. Minis Hays, Philadelphia.

GEORGE THOMPSON

Israel B. Kursheedt, 1776–1852. Painted 1842.
  Owned by the Misses Kursheedt, New York.

ELKANAH TISDALE

Major Mordecai Myers, 1776–1870. Miniature.
  This miniature is reproduced in "Biographical Sketches of the Bailey-Myers-
  Mason Families, 1776–1905."

BENJAMIN TROTT

Benjamin I. Cohen, 1797–1845. Miniature, 4 x 5 inches. Attributed to
  Trott.
Solomon Etting, 1764–1847. Miniature. 2½ x 4½ inches (profile).
  Attributed to Trott.
Solomon Etting, 1764–1847. Miniature, 2½ x 4½ inches (facing front).
  Attributed to Trott.
Joseph Solomon, 1700–1780. Miniature, 1½ x 4½ inches. Attributed
  to Trott.

  These miniatures are in the Collection of the Maryland Historical
    Society.

JOHN WOLLASTON

Mrs. Isaac Mendes Seixas (Rachel Levy), 1710–1797. Attributed to Wollaston by Lawrence Park.
Owned by Hon. N. Taylor Phillips, New York.

JOSEPH WOOD

Samuel Etting, ?–?. Miniature. Attributed to Wood.
  Owned by the Pennsylvania Academy of Fine Arts.

UNKNOWN ARTISTS

Abrahams, ?–?.
Owned by Samuel Ewing, Esq., Philadelphia, Pa.

Abraham Alexander, 1771–1844.
There is a reproduction of this portrait in *The New Age*, a Masonic publication. February, 1907.

Joseph Andrews. Living in Philadelphia, 1804.
Owned by Mrs. E. L. Goldbaum, Memphis, Tenn.

Mrs. Joseph Andrews (Sallie Salomon), 1779–1854. Daughter of Haym
Salomon.
Owned by Mrs. E. L. Goldbaum, Memphis, Tenn.

Mrs. Mathias Bush (Becky Meyers or Mears), ?–?. Miniature.
There is a photograph of this miniature in the possession of Miss Mordecai, Philadelphia, Pa.

Mrs. Benjamin I. Cohen (Kitty Etting), 1799–1837. Miniature.
Collection of the Maryland Historical Society.

Jacob Cohen, 1741–1808.
Owned by J. Quintus Cohen, Esq., New York.
See reproduction in "Jews of South Carolina," by Dr. Barnett A. Elzas.

Jacob Cohen, 1792–1858.
Owned by Mrs. Alexander Hart, Norfolk, Va.

Mordecai Cohen, 1763–1848. 25 x 30 inches. Half-length.
Owned by Mrs. Francis D. Pollack, New York.

Mrs. Mordecai Cohen (Leah Lazarus). 25 x 30 inches. Half-length.
Owned by Mrs. Francis D. Pollack, New York.
Mrs. Pollack writes that the Cohen portraits were painted by Theodore S. Moise and either John or Joshua Cantor, but it is not known who painted which!

Mrs. Solomon Myers Cohen (Belle Simon).
Owned by Henry Joseph, Esq., Montreal, Canada.

Lorenzo Da Ponte, 1749–1837.
Owned by Columbia University, New York.

Jacob De Leon. Living in Kingston, Jamaica, 1790. Miniature.
Owned by Bunford Samuel, Esq., Philadelphia, Pa.

Unknown Artists (*Continued*)

Esther Andrews Dreyfous. Painted in 1828, with baby daughter in her
    arms. Granddaughter of Haym Salomon.
    Owned by Miss Gertrude Dreyfous, New York.

Mrs. Solomon Etting (Rachel Gratz), 1764–1831. Miniature.
    Collection of the Maryland Historical Society.

David Franks, 1720–1793, and Phila Franks, as children.
    Owned by Hon. N. Taylor Phillips, New York.
    There are two portraits of David with his sister Phila, as children, in this col-
    lection.

Jacob Franks, 1688–1769.
    Owned by Hon. N. Taylor Phillips, New York.

Mrs. Jacob Franks (Bilhah Abigail Levy), 1700 (?)–1750 (?).
    Owned by Hon. N. Taylor Phillips, New York.

Phila Franks, 1722–?. As a young lady.
    Owned by Hon. N. Taylor Phillips, New York.

Rebecca Franks, 1758–1823. Painted by an English artist.
    This portrait is reproduced in a pamphlet on "The Jewish Woman in Amer-
    ica," by Leon Huhner, A.M., LL.B.

Rebecca Franks. Painted 1775.
    Owned by Mrs. Clarence I. De Sola, Montreal.

Aaron Lopez Gomez, ?–1860.
    Owned by Edgar J. Nathan, Esq., New York.

Benjamin Gomez, 1711–1772. Miniature.
    Owned by Edgar J. Nathan, Esq., New York.

Isaac Gomez, Jr., 1768–1831 (?). Son of Moses and Esther Gomez.
    There is a photograph of this portrait in the collection of the American Jewish
    Historical Society, New York.

Aaron Hart, 1724–1800. One of first Jewish Free Masons in America.
    Certificate of membership dated New York, June 10, 1760.
    Settled in Canada.
    This portrait is reproduced in "The Jew in Canada," by Arthur Daniel Hart.

Alexander Hart, ?–1838.
    Owned by Mrs. Alexander Hart, Norfolk, Va.

Bernard Hart, 1764–1855. A founder of New York Stock Exchange and
its secretary for many years.
Owned by estate of the late Theodore Myers, New York.
This portrait is reproduced in "The Life of Bret Harte," by H. C. Merwin,
Boston, 1911. For some time the portrait hung in the offices of Messrs. Arthur
Lipper & Co., New York, but at the present time it is probably in the posses-
sion of Mr. Myers' widow, Mrs. Benn V. La Rue, New York.

Daniel Hart, ?–?. Miniature.
Owned by Miss Isabel Cohen, New York.

Mrs. Daniel Hart, ?–?. Miniature.
Owned by Miss Isabel Cohen, New York.

Barrah (?) Hays, ?–?.
A photograph of this portrait is in the possession of the American Jewish Historical Society, New York.

Mrs. Isaac Hays (Rebecca Judah), ?–?.
Owned by Miss Mordecai, Philadelphia, Pa.

Moses Michael Hays, 1738–1805. Father of Judah Hays, whose portrait
was painted by Stuart.
A copy of the original portrait, which has been destroyed, is in the Masonic
Temple, Boston.

Uriah Hendricks, ?–?. Married 1826.
Owned by Henry S. Hendricks, New York.

Mrs. Uriah Hendricks (Fanny Tobias), ?–?.
Owned by Henry S. Hendricks, New York.

Joshua Isaacs, ?–1810.
Owned by Mrs. Beatrice Phillips, New York.

Mrs. Joshua Isaacs (Brandly Lazarus), ?–?.
Owned by Mrs. Beatrice Phillips, New York.

Moses Isaacks, 1727–1798.
Owned by Dr. Francis Allen De Ford, Philadelphia.

Israel Israel, 1743–1821.
Owned by Arthur G. Ellet, Esq., Kansas City.

Mrs. Israel Israel (Hannah Erwin), 1757–1813.
Owned by Arthur G. Ellet, Esq., Kansas City.

UNKNOWN ARTISTS (*Continued*)

Israel Israel, 1743–1821. Pastel.
Owned by Mrs. James Alden Valentine, Walpole, Mass.

Mrs. Israel Israel (Hannah Erwin), ?–?. Pastel.
Owned by Mrs. James Alden Valentine, Walpole, Mass.

Israel Israel, 1743–1821.
Grand Master's Room, Masonic Temple, Philadelphia, Pa.

Israel Jacobs, 1714–1810.
Collection of the American Jewish Historical Society, New York.

Myer Jacobs, ?–?. Lived in Charleston, S. C. Painted about 1815.
There is a photograph of this portrait in the possession of Dr. Barnett A. Elzas, New York.

Naphtali Judah, 1774–?.
This portrait is reproduced in a Masonic publication—"Robert W. Reid, Washington Lodge, No. 21, A. F. and A. M., New York, 1911."

Rabbi Raphael Haijm Karigal, 1733–1778. Lived in Newport, 1775.
Owned by MacGregor Jenkins, Esq., Dover, Mass.

Aaron Levy, 1742–1815. Miniature.
Owned by Dr. A. S. W. Rosenbach, New York.

Aaron Levy, 1742–1815.
Owned by the Clay family, Lexington, Ky.

Mrs. Aaron Levy (Rachel (?), ?–?.
Owned by J. Bunford Samuel, Esq., Philadelphia, Pa.

Abraham Levy, ?–?.
Owned by Herbert T. Ezekiel, Esq., Richmond, Va.

Mrs. Abraham Levy (Rachel Barnard). Painted 1835.
Owned by Herbert T. Ezekiel, Esq., Richmond, Va.

Moses Levy, 1665–1728.
Owned by Hon. N. Taylor Phillips, New York.

Samson Levy, Sr., 1723–1781. Miniature.
This miniature was formerly owned by Mr. Frank Adams, of Philadelphia. It is now possibly in the possession of his descendant, Robert Adams, Philadelphia.

Zipporah Levy, 1760–1832.
Owned by Hon. N. Taylor Phillips, New York.

Aaron Lopez, 1731–1782.
This portrait has been reproduced in "Publications of the American Jewish Historical Society," Vol. 27.

David Lopez. Lived in Charleston, S. C. Painted about 1800.
A photograph is in the possession of Dr. Barnett A. Elzas, New York.

Sarah Lopez (Mrs. Aaron Lopez) and son Joshua, ?–?.
A photographic copy is in the possession of the American Jewish Historical Society, New York.

Jacob Lyon, 1777–1851.
A photograph of the original portrait is in the possession of Mrs. Louisa B. Lapin, Harrisonburg, Va.

Solomon Marache. Living in Philadelphia 1760. Miniature.
Owned by Rev. Bent, Philadelphia, Pa.

Solomon Marache. Living in Philadelphia 1760.
Owned by Mrs. George Knox M. McIlwain, Philadelphia, Pa.

Mrs. Solomon Marache, ?–?.
Owned by Mrs. George Knox M. McIlwain, Philadelphia, Pa.

Isaac C. Moses, ?–1834. Miniature.
Miss Eleanor S. Cohen, of Baltimore, possesses a photographic copy of this miniature.

I. S. Moss, ?–?.
Owned by the Jewish Maternity Hospital, Philadelphia.

John Moss, 1771–1847.
Owned by Frank Samuel, Esq., Philadelphia.

Samuel Myers, 1775–1836. Miniature.
Owned by Mrs. Edward Cohen, Washington, D. C.

Major Benjamin Nones, 1757–1826.
Owned by Walter M. Nones, Esq., Long Island City, New York.

Mrs. Benjamin Nones (Miriam Marks), 1764–1822.
Owned by Walter M. Nones, Esq., Long Island City, New York.

Jacob Philadelphia, ?–1735.
A photographic copy from his portrait is in the possession of the American Jewish Historical Society.

Aaron Phillips, ?–1826.
Owned by Hon. N. Taylor Phillips, New York.

Deborah Salomon, ?–1808. Pastel. Daughter of Haym Salomon.
Owned by Mrs. Maria Moss, Brookline, Mass.

UNKNOWN ARTISTS (*Continued*)

Mrs. Philip Schuyler (Shinah Simon), ?–?. Wax portrait.
Owned by Henry Joseph, Esq., Montreal, Canada.

Capt. Abraham Seixas, 1759–1799.
Owned by the Congregation Shearith Israel, New York.
This portrait is reproduced in the "Jews of South Carolina," by Dr. Barnett A. Elzas.

Rev. Gershom Mendes Seixas, 1745–1816. Miniature.
Owned by Mrs. Annie Nathan Meyer, New York.

Rev. Gershom Mendes Seixas, 1745–1816.
A reproduction of a bas-relief of Mr. Seixas appears in the "Historical Sketch of the Congregation Mikve Israel," by Dr. A. S. W. Rosenbach.

Rachel Hannah Seixas, 1773–?. Miniature.
Owned by Hon. N. Taylor Phillips, New York.

Mordecai Sheftall, 1735–1797. Miniature.
Owned by Edmund H. Abrahams, Esq., Savannah, Ga.

Mrs. Mordecai Sheftall (Frances Hart). Living in Charleston, S. C.,
1779. Miniature.
Owned by Edmund H. Abrahams, Esq., Savannah, Ga.

Sheftall Sheftall, ?–1848. Son of Mordecai Sheftall. Woodcarving.
A reproduction may be found in White's "Historical Collections of Georgia."

Joseph Simon, 1712–1804. Silhouette.
Owned by Henry Joseph, Esq., Montreal, Canada.

Levy Solomons. Maintained a home in Albany, New York, but lived for
the most part in Canada.
This portrait is reproduced in "The Jew in Canada," by Arthur Daniel Hart.

Judah Touro, 1775–1854.
Owned by the Redwood Library, Newport, R. I.

Judah Touro, 1775–1854.
Touro Infirmary, New Orleans, La.

Judah Touro, 1775–1854. Water Color.
Owned by Amelia Kursheedt, New Orleans, La.

BIBLIOGRAPHY

BIDDLE, EDWARD, and MANTLE FIELDING. Life and Works of Thomas Sully. Philadelphia, 1922.

BOLTON, CHARLES KNOWLES. The Founders. Boston, 1919.

BOLTON, ETHEL STANWOOD. Wax Portraits and Silhouettes. Boston, 1915.

BOLTON, THEODORE. Early American Portrait Painters in Miniature. New York, 1921.

DUNLAP, WILLIAM. History of the Arts of Design in the United States. Edited by Bayley and Goodspeed. Boston, 1918.

ELLET, E. F. Women of the American Revolution. Vol. I. New York, 1848.

ELZAS, DR. BARNETT A. The Jews of South Carolina. Philadelphia, 1905.

EZEKIEL, HERBERT T., and LICHTENSTEIN, GASTON. The History of the Jews of Richmond. Richmond, 1917.

FEVRET DE SAINT-MÉMIN, CHARLES B. J. The St.-Mémin Collection of Portraits. New York, 1862.

HART, ARTHUR DANIEL. The Jew in Canada. Toronto, 1926.

HOLMES, ABIEL. Life of Ezra Stiles. Boston, 1798.

ISHAM, SAMUEL. History of American Painting. New York, 1905.

JEWISH ENCYCLOPEDIA.

LITERARY DIARY OF EZRA STILES, PRESIDENT OF YALE COLLEGE. Yale Corporation. New York, 1901.

MARKENS, ISAAC. The Hebrews in America. New York, 1888.

MASON, GEORGE C. Life and Works of Gilbert Stuart. New York, 1879.

MORAIS, HENRY S. The Jews of Philadelphia. Philadelphia, 1892.

PARK, LAWRENCE. Gilbert Stuart. William Edwin Rudge, New York, 1926.

PUBLICATIONS OF THE AMERICAN JEWISH HISTORICAL SOCIETY, Vols. 1–27.

SULLY, THOMAS. Register of Portraits painted by Thomas Sully, 1801–1871. Edited by Charles Henry Hart, Philadelphia, 1909.

TUCKERMAN, HENRY T. Book of the Artists. New York, 1867.

WHARTON, ANNE H. Heirlooms in Miniature. Philadelphia, 1898.

WHARTON, ANNE H. Salons Colonial and Republican. Philadelphia, 1900.

PLATES

JACOB FRANKS

Owned by Hon. N. Taylor Phillips, New York

MRS. JACOB FRANKS

Owned by Hon. N. Taylor Phillips, New York

DAVID AND PHILA FRANKS

Owned by Hon. N. Taylor Phillips, New York

PHILA FRANKS

Owned by Hon. N. Taylor Phillips, New York

MOSES LEVY

Owned by Hon. N. Taylor Phillips, New York

MRS. ISAAC MENDES SEIXAS

Attributed to JOHN WOLLASTON

Owned by Hon. N. Taylor Phillips, New York

RABBI RAPHAEL HAIJM KARIGAL

Owned by MacGregor Jenkins, Esq., Dover, Mass.

EZRA STILES
(*Friend of the Jews*)
SAMUEL KING

MOSES MICHAEL HAYS

Masonic Temple, Boston

ISRAEL JACOBS

Owned by the American Jewish Historical Society

JONAS PHILLIPS

Attributed to CHARLES WILLSON PEALE

Owned by the American Jewish Historical Society

MRS. JONAS PHILLIPS

Attributed to CHARLES WILLSON PEALE

Owned by Isaac Graff, Esq., New York

COMMODORE URIAH P. LEVY

Attributed to THOMAS BUCHANAN READ

Thomas Jefferson Home, Monticello, Va.

JUDGE MOSES LEVY

REMBRANDT PEALE

Owned by J. J. Milligan, Esq., Baltimore

ISRAEL ISRAEL

Owned by Arthur G. Ellet, Esq., Kansas City

MRS. ISRAEL ISRAEL
Owned by Arthur G. Ellet, Esq., Kansas City

MRS. AARON LEVY

Owned by J. Bunford Samuel, Esq., Philadelphia

JOHN MOSS

Attributed to WILLIAM HENRY BROWN

Owned by J. Bunford Samuel, Esq., Philadelphia

MANUEL JOSEPHSON

JEREMIAH THEUS

Owned by Dr. I. Minis Hays, Philadelphia

MRS. MANUEL JOSEPHSON

JEREMIAH THEUS

Owned by Dr. I. Minis Hays, Philadelphia

BARNARD GRATZ

CHARLES PEALE POLK

Owned by Dr. I. Minis Hays, Philadelphia

MRS. BARNARD GRATZ

Attributed to ROBERT FEKE

Owned by Dr. I. Minis Hays, Philadelphia

JOSEPH ANDREWS

Owned by Mrs. E. L. Goldbaum, Memphis

MRS. JOSEPH ANDREWS
Owned by Mrs. E. L. Goldbaum, Memphis

MORDECAI MANUEL NOAH

MAJOR MORDECAI MYERS

John Wesley Jarvis

MRS. SOLOMON ETTING

John Wesley Jarvis

Owned by the Maryland Historical Society

SOLOMON ETTING

John Wesley Jarvis

Owned by the Maryland Historical Society

MRS. SAMSON LEVY, SR.

FEVRET DE ST. MÉMIN

Owned by Mrs. Robert Hale Bancroft, Boston

SAMSON LEVY, JR.

FEVRET DE ST. MÉMIN

Owned by Mrs. Robert Hale Bancroft, Boston

COLONEL DAVID SALISBURY FRANKS

CHARLES WILLSON PEALE

Owned by Mrs. Clarence I. De Sola, Montreal

JACOB DE LEON

Owned by Bunford Samuel, Esq., Philadelphia

ISAAC C. MOSES

RACHEL (GRATZ) ETTING

Owned by the Maryland Historical Society

SOLOMON ETTING

Attributed to BENJAMIN TROTT

Owned by the Maryland Historical Society

BENJAMIN I. COHEN

Attributed to BENJAMIN TROTT

Owned by the Maryland Historical Society

JOSEPH SOLOMON
Attributed to BENJAMIN TROTT
Owned by the Maryland Historical Society

MIRIAM (ETTING) MYERS

Edward Greene Malbone

Owned by the Maryland Historical Society

RACHEL GRATZ
EDWARD GREENE MALBONE
Owned by Mrs. John Hunter, Savannah, Ga.

REBECCA GRATZ
EDWARD GREENE MALBONE
Owned by Miss Rachel Gratz Nathan, New York

JACOB RODRIGUEZ RIVERA

GILBERT STUART

Owned by the Redwood Library, Newport

SAMUEL MYERS

GILBERT STUART

Owned by Mrs. John Hill Morgan, Brooklyn

JUDAH HAYS
Gilbert Stuart
Owned by Mrs. William C. Preston, Richmond, Va.

MOSES MYERS

GILBERT STUART

Owned by Barton Myers, Esq., Norfolk, Va.

MRS. MOSES MYERS

<small>Gilbert Stuart</small>

Owned by Barton Myers, Esq., Norfolk, Va.

—◦◦❧{ 165 }❧◦◦—

COLONEL ISAAC FRANKS

GILBERT STUART

Owned by the Pennsylvania Academy of Fine Arts

MRS. SOLOMON MOSES

GILBERT STUART

Owned by Henry Joseph, Esq., Montreal

SOLOMON MOSES

GILBERT STUART

Owned by Henry Joseph, Esq., Montreal

MRS. MICHAEL GRATZ

GILBERT STUART

Owned by Henry Joseph, Esq., Montreal

JOSEPH GRATZ

GEORGE P. A. HEALY

Owned by Henry Joseph, Esq., Montreal

REBECCA GRATZ

THOMAS SULLY

Owned by Henry Joseph, Esq., Montreal

MICHAEL GRATZ

Thomas Sully

Owned by Henry Joseph, Esq., Montreal

GUSTAVUS A. MYERS

THOMAS SULLY

Owned by Mrs. John Hill Morgan, Brooklyn

FANNY (YATES) LEVY

THOMAS SULLY

Owned by the Corcoran Gallery of Art

MAJOR ALFRED MORDECAI

From pencil sketch by KATES *of portrait by* THOMAS SULLY
Owned by Miss Mordecai, Philadelphia

SOLOMON JACOBS

Thomas Sully

Owned by Mrs. William A. Harriman, New York

SAMSON LEVY, JR.

THOMAS SULLY

Owned by Mrs. Robert Hale Bancroft, Boston

INDEX

INDEX

INDEX